STEP-BY-STEP INSTRUCTIONS AND FULL SIZE PATTERNS

101 BEAUTIFUL
FELT FLOWERS

PIENI SIENI

Tuva

Contents

INTRODUCTION

The flowers in this book are all made with felt. This material is easy to find and exists in a wide variety of colors. The techniques are simple, and the creations look almost like real flowers. The models are all on a stem to help with customization. Choose any of the 101 flowers of all sizes. Cut, glue, and sew the felt components to make your favorite flowers.

Variation 1

A brooch

Attach a brooch pin to the stem of a flower to transform it into a brooch (see p. 41).

Variation 2

In a bud vase

The models are all on a stem so they may be placed in a vase.

Variation 3

A bouquet

Create your own bouquet and hold it together with a pretty ribbon.

Blue Flowers

Blue is such a relaxing color. Delicate and elegant, these small flowers are created in a variety of blues for a soft, peaceful ambiance.

6

Instructions

10-a

10-b

Yellow Flowers

Their bubbly color will instantly boost
your mood.
The small flowers on p.9 are perfect to
customize bags or clothing.

Instructions

Romantic Flowers

Their layers of petals grant these five
flowers their elegance and femininity.
They are incredibly romantic.

How to Make

29-a

29-b

29-c

29-d

Red Flowers

Red flowers are the most common flowers in a florist's shop. Make them to celebrate a milestone, or simply to say I love you.

Instructions

Wild Flowers

The small, colorful, discreet flowers growing on the side of the road can become the focus point of a trendy decoration.

Instructions

41-a

42-a

*Primula
polyanthus*

43-b

43-a

*Lobularia
maritima*

44-a 44-b

*Lobelia
erinus*

*Tristagma
uniflorum*

45-a *Trifolium
repens*

46-a

42-b

47-a

*Primula
polyanthus*

*Armeria
maritima*

47-b

45-b *Trifolium
pratense*

Nemesia

41-b

*Tristagma
uniflorum*

46-b

48-a 48-b

49-a

49-b

50-a

50-b

51-a

Nemesia

Isotoma

*Lewisia
cotyledon*

*Silene
armeria*

51-b

Oxalis

52-a

52-b

53-a

53-b

54-a

54-b

Geranium

Lotera

*Astrantia
major*

15

55-a

55-b

57-a

57-b

56

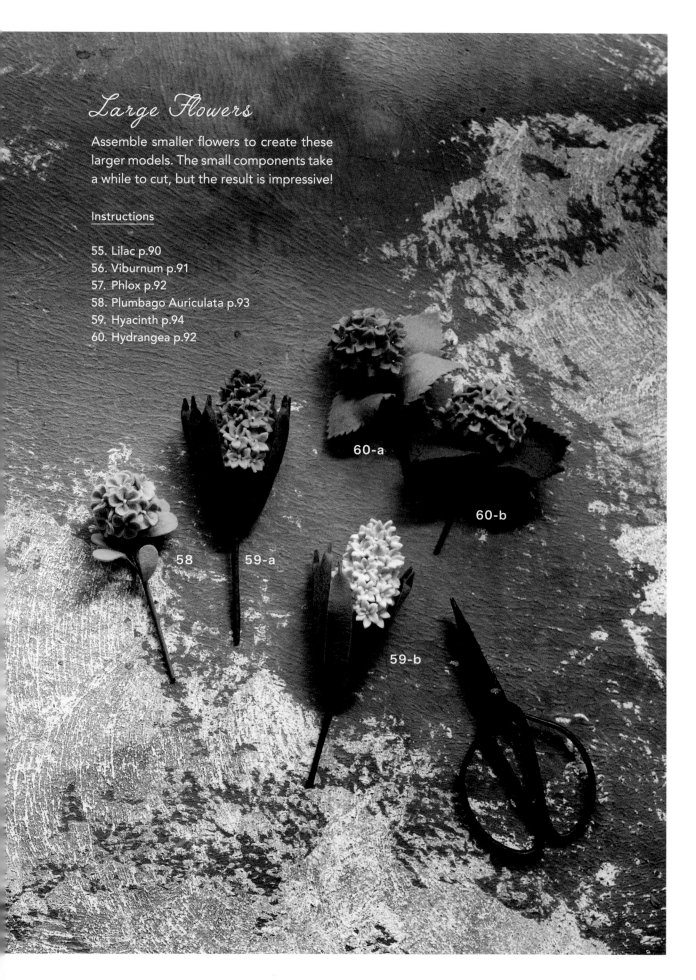

Large Flowers

Assemble smaller flowers to create these larger models. The small components take a while to cut, but the result is impressive!

Instructions

60-a

60-b

58

59-a

59-b

Violets

These flowers let us know Spring is here. The viola is a monochrome creation, while the pansy and violet are both multicolored.

61-b

61-c

61-a

62-b

62-a

63

Slender Flowers

Roll up a length of notched felt to create these flowers. Their rustic look will enhance the charm of any bouquet.

Instructions

Poppies and Buttercups

These elegant, refined flowers feature large petals.
They will look amazing in your decor.

21

74

73-a

73-b

75

72-a

72-b

77-a

77-b

76-a

76-b

Asterales

Fine, dense petals characterize the flowers in this family. Cut the petals delicately to create these flowers.

Instructions

78-b

78-a

Large Flowers of the Asterales Family

These large flowers will offer a welcome presence and work within almost any style of decor.

Instructions

84-b

84-a

85-a

85-b

86

87

Specific Shaped Flowers

These four flowers all have a distinct appearance, but they are created from the same components combined with clever placement.

Rose

The queen of the flowers, the rose, is represented here in 5 variations. Which is your favorite?

White Flowers

White flowers symbolize purity and softness. Whether bell shaped like the lily of the valley, or with curved petals like the calla, they are all equally pretty. Only the techniques change.

97

98

99

100

101

a

b

d

e

c

Brooches

Floral Bouquets

Assemble a few different flowers to create
these colorful, charming bouquets! Tone
on tone, in different shades of a color, in
pastels, or in bright colors, the possibilities
are endless.

Instructions: p.142 • 143

Various Jewels

*Tutorials not included.

Jewels for the Ear

Assemble a few flowers and wrap floral ribbon around the stems. Curve the stem to follow the shape of the ear.

Comb

Glue flowers of various sizes to a hair comb.

Necklace

Assemble a few flowers and make a ring on either side. Attach a chain to create a stunning flower necklace.

Basic Techniques

27 techniques are used in this book. Most of the models are made using a combination of these techniques. Learn these techniques before starting on the flowers.

Thread of a contrasting color is used in these tutorials. Choose a thread color that matches the felt color when making the flowers.

A-1. Beaded flower heart with 1 strand of steel wire

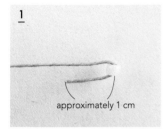

Thread a bead onto a length of steel wire. Fold at 1 cm of end.

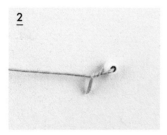

Twist the steel wire 2 or 3 times close to the bead.

Cut the end of the steel wire.

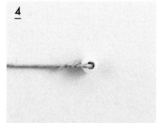

The beaded flower heart with 1 strand of steel wire is finished.

A-2. Beaded flower heart with 2 strands of steel wire

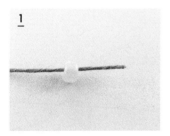

Thread a bead onto a length of steel wire.

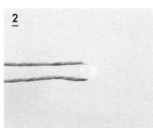

Fold steel wire in 2.

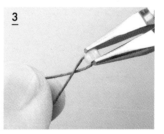

Hold the bead with pliers and twist the steel wire 2 or 3 times close to the bead.

The beaded flower heart with 2 strands of steel wire is finished.

B. Threading a wooden bead

B-1 Bead + wooden bead

B-2 Bead + wooden bead
(twisting the wire)

B-3 Wooden bead

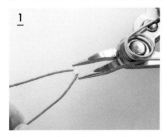

Thread 1 bead onto 1 length of steel wire. Hold the bead with pliers and fold the steel wire in 2.

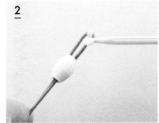

Thread 1 wooden bead onto the 2 strands of steel wire and glue it in place.

Thread 1 bead onto 1 length of steel wire. Twist the steel wire 2 or 3 times close to the bead. Thread a wooden bead and glue it in place.

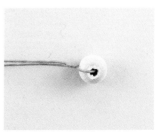

Thread 1 wooden bead onto 1 length of steel wire. Fold the steel wire in 2, then twist the steel wire 2 or 3 times close to the bead.

C. Wooden bead covered in petals

※The number of petals may vary by project.

C-1
4-petal corolla

Punch 1 hole in the centre of the corolla. Insert a length of steel wire into the hole. Apply glue to petals.

Glue petals around the wooden bead.

C-2
5-petal corolla

Punch 1 hole in the centre of the corolla. Insert a length of steel wire into the hole. Apply glue to 1 petal.

Glue petal to the wooden bead.

Glue the rest of the petals one by one.

C-3
8-petal corolla

Punch 1 hole in the centre of the corolla. Insert a length of steel wire into the hole. Apply glue to opposite petals.

Glue these petals to the wooden bead.

Apply glue to the remaining petals and glue to the wooden bead.

D. Gluing the steel wire to a leaf

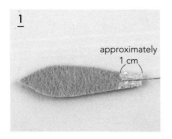

approximately 1 cm

Apply glue to the bottom of a leaf and place a length of steel wire on top.

Pinch the bottom of the leaf to glue together.

Hold the pinched portion in place with a clamp and leave to dry.

The steel wire is glued to a leaf.

E. Inserting the steel wire into a leaf

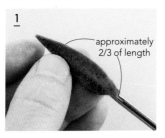
1

approximately 2/3 of length

Insert the punch needle into the felt about 2/3 of the leaf's length.

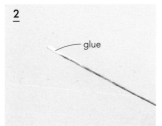
2

glue

Apply glue to the end of the steel wire.

3

Insert the steel wire into the hole from step 1.

4

Leave to dry.

F. Tightening the corolla

F-1 1 Corolla

1

Thread the needle and make a stop knot. Insert needle from back to front.

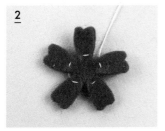
2

Sew around the centre of the corolla.

3

Stitch into the 1st stitch.

4

Pull the thread to tighten. Secure with 1 stitch and 1 stop knot on the wrong side.

F-2 Overlaid corollas

1

Cut two identical pieces.

2

Place one top of the other then stitch around the centre of the corollas. Stitch into the 1st stitch to end.

3

Pull the thread to tighten. Secure with 1 stitch and 1 stop knot on the wrong side.

F-3 Sewing beads

1

Sew 1 bead to the bottom of each petal using the forward stitch.

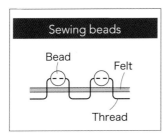

Sewing beads

Bead

Felt

Thread

2

At the end of the round, stitch into the 1st stitch and send the needle out on the wrong side.

3

Pull the thread to tighten. Secure with 1 stitch and 1 stop knot on the wrong side.

G. Notched and tightened felt　　※Some components will be notched but not tightened.

G-1 Single component

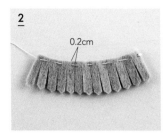

1	2	3	4
Cut 1 long side with notching scissors. Notch at inner angles.	Sew along the unnotched side, 0.2 cm from the edge.	Stitch into the 1st stitch to form a ring.	Pull the thread to tighten. Secure with 1 stitch and 1 stop knot on the wrong side.

G-2 Folded components

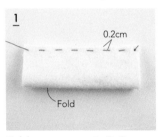

1	2	3	4
Fold component in 2. Sew 0.2 cm from the edge.	Notch the component at regular intervals. If the component is not tightened, secure with 1 stitch.	Stitch into the 1st stitch to form a ring.	Pull the thread to tighten. Secure with 1 stitch and 1 stop knot on the wrong side.

H. Rolling up a component

1	2	3	4
Prepare the component.	Roll up starting from one side, aligning the edge.	Sew bottom of the piece in a cross shape.	The component is rolled up.

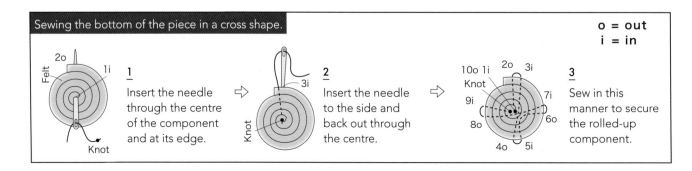

Sewing the bottom of the piece in a cross shape.　　o = out　i = in

1 Insert the needle through the centre of the component and at its edge.

2 Insert the needle to the side and back out through the centre.

3 Sew in this manner to secure the rolled-up component.

I. Overlock stitch

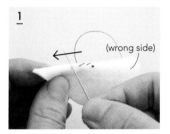
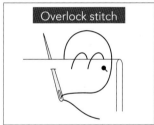
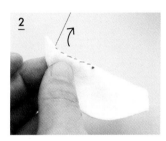
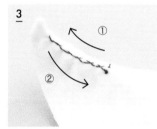

Fold component in 2, with right sides facing each other. Sew along the fold using the overlock stitch, making sure the stitches are not visible on the right side of the work.

Sew as indicated in the template. Pull thread upward.

Sew in the opposite direction, still using the overlock stitch, back to the starting point. Secure with 1 stitch.

J. Attaching the steel wire to a component that is folded in 2

Fold twice

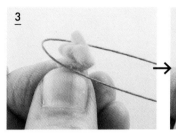

Fold component in 2.

Fold component in 2 again.

Fold the steel wire in 2 and place it in a groove of the folded component.

Twist the steel wire 2 or 3 times at the bottom of the component.

Fold once

Fold component and steel wire in 2. Place the wire in a groove of the folded component. Twist the steel wire 2 or 3 times at the bottom of the component.

K. Making a circular support with steel wire

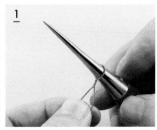
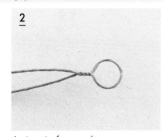

Roll the middle of the length of steel wire around a punch needle. Twist the wire 2 or 3 times at the base of the punch needle.

A ring is formed.

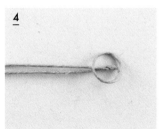

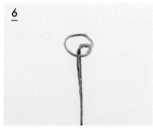

Fold the ring with pliers.

The ring is folded.

Pinch the twisted portion, then fold the steel wire at a 90-degree angle.

The circular support is complete.

L. Rolling up a component around the steel wire

1
Fold the component in 2. Sew the edge and notch the fold (see technique G-2, steps 1 and 2). Fold the steel wire in 2, then place it on the notched side at one end.

2
Hold together with pliers.

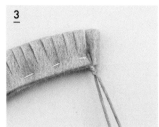

3
Twist the steel wire 2 or 3 times at the bottom of the component.

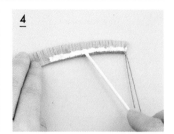

4
Apply glue to 1/3 of the component on the unnotched edge.

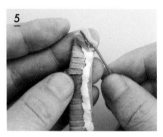

5
Roll up the component around the steel wire in a spiral.

6
Stop at the end of the portion with glue on it.

7
Apply glue to 1/3 of the component, then continue as per steps 4 to 6.

8
Repeat to roll up all the way to the end.

M. Ruffled component

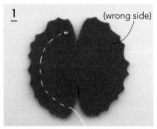

1
(wrong side)
(right side)
Sew using the forward stitch, making sure the stitches are not visible on the right side.

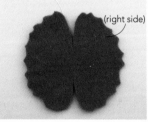

2
(wrong side)
Pull the thread, then secure with 1 knot.

3
Ruffle the other side in the same manner.

N. Pinched component

1
Apply glue to the end of the petal.

2
Fold in 2 and hold in place with a clamp.

3
Glue the end of the remaining petals in the same manner.

4
Once dry, remove the clamps.

O. Assembled and rolled-up components

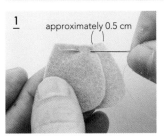

1 approximately 0.5 cm

Overlay 2 components, staggering the edges. Sew using the forward stitch.

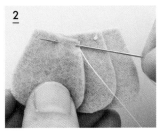

2

Overlay another component on top of the ones from step 1 and continue sewing.

3

Overlay the remaining components, sewing them using the forward stitch.

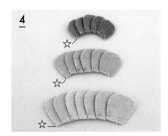

4

Assemble the other components in the same manner.

5

Start to roll up the maroon component, starting at the edge marked with a ☆ in the step 4 photo.

6

Roll up aligning the edge.

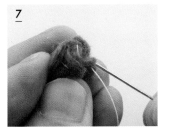

7

Sew the bottom of the component in a cross shape (see p. 36, H technique).

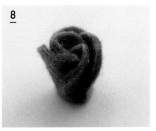

8

The middle component is finished.

9

Roll up the intermediate component from step 4 around the middle component from step 8.

10

Roll up the outer component in the same manner. Sew the bottom in a cross shape.

P. Creating a cup

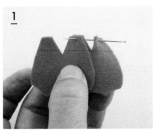

1

Overlap the ends of two petals.

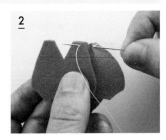

2

Pull the thread and insert the needle in the same place as in step 1.

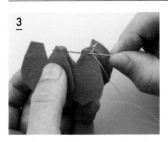

3

Overlap another petal on the component from step 2 and sew.

4

Continue in this manner with the remaining petals. Overlap the ends as well.

5

Sew as in steps 1 and 2, then secure with 1 knot.

6

The petals form a cup.

Q. Gluing embroidery thread to the steel wire

1

Cut the embroidery thread into small pieces.

2

Cut enough thread.

3

Apply glue to the end of the steel wire, then glue the pieces of embroidery thread.

4

Leave to dry.

R. Inserting the steel wire through a corolla

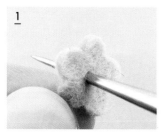
1

Punch a hole in the centre of the corolla.

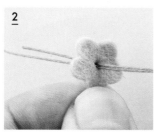
2

Insert the steel wire in this hole.

> This technique is also used to create the chalice.

S. Using floral ribbon

1

Prepare approximately 15 to 20 cm of floral ribbon.

2

Stretch it to increase its adherence.

3

Place the wire on the end of the ribbon.

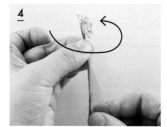
4

Hold the end of the ribbon in place with your fingers and turn the wire, pulling the ribbon down.

5

Join remaining wires if needed, continuing to wrap the ribbon around them.

6

Cut excess steel wire.

7

Cover the ends of the wire with floral ribbon.

8

Press on the end of the stem to secure the ribbon.

Making the Template and Cutting the Components

Place thick tracing paper on the template. Trace the shape with a pen.

Cut the tracing.

Punch a hole in any markers, such as the end of a notch. The template is finished.

Place the template onto the felt. Trace with a marker pencil.

Also trace any markers.

Cut the felt.

Notch through to the markers.

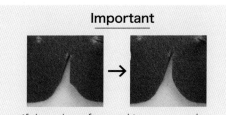

Important

If the edge of a petal is not smooth, cut again delicately to give it a natural curve.

The component is cut.

※Felt does not have a right or wrong side.

Attaching a Brooch Pin

It is possible to attach a brooch pin to create an accessory.

Assemble the stems and wrap them in floral ribbon.

Open the brooch pin and place it on the back of the stems. Wrap floral ribbon around the stem and the brooch pin.

The brooch pin is secured with floral ribbon. If it is attached far from the flowers, these may bend because of their weight.

Assemble the leaves and continue to wrap in floral ribbon.

Cut excess steel wire and finish wrapping in floral ribbon all the way to the end.

Creating the Projects and Reading the Instructions

Steps

Most of the creations are made in this order: heart, flower, bud, leaf, assembly.
The Myosotis from p. 6 is explained step-by-step as an example.

How to read the instructions:

The letters correspond to a technique explained from pages 32 to 40.

1. Myosotis P. 6

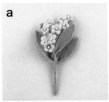
a

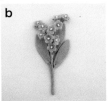
b

Supplies
(from left to right: models a/b)

Felt
10 x 2 cm x 2 cm pieces light blue/purple (corollas)
3 x 2 cm x 6 cm pieces green (leaves)

Other supplies (for each model)
10 x 0.3 cm light yellow beads (hearts)
10 x 36 cm lengths of 0.3 mm steel wire (flowers)
3 x 18 cm lengths of 0.3 mm steel wire (leaves)
Green floral ribbon

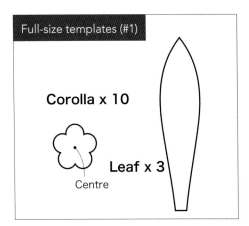

Full-size templates (#1)

Corolla x 10

Centre

Leaf x 3

1 Make the hearts.

A-2 (see p. 33)

Thread 1 bead onto 1 length of steel wire. Twist the wire 2 or 3 times close to the bead.

2 Make the flowers.

R (see p. 40)

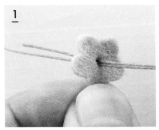
1

Punch 1 hole in the centre of the corolla. Insert the wire from step 1 into the hole.

2

Apply glue to the bottom of the bead and glue it to the corolla.

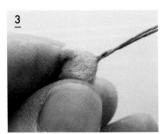
3

Press on the corolla to shape it.

4

1 flower is finished. Make 9 more flowers in the same manner.

3 Make the leaves.
D (see p. 34)

Apply glue to the bottom of the leaf. Place 1 length of wire on it and fold the bottom of the leaf to glue together. Make 3 leaves.

4 Assemble the flowers.

1

Join 3 flowers and wrap floral ribbon around them.

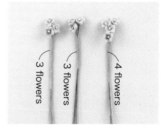

Make 2 components with 3 flowers each and 1 component with 4 flowers.

5 Assemble the flowers and the leaves.   S (see p. 40)

1

Join the flowers from step 4-2 and wrap floral ribbon around them.

2

Join 1 leaf and continue wrapping in floral ribbon.

3

Join the 2 remaining leaves and continue wrapping in floral ribbon. Cut excess wire.

4

Cover the ends of the wire with floral ribbon.

5

The finished work.

The measurements are approximate. They represent the total length and the length of the flowers.

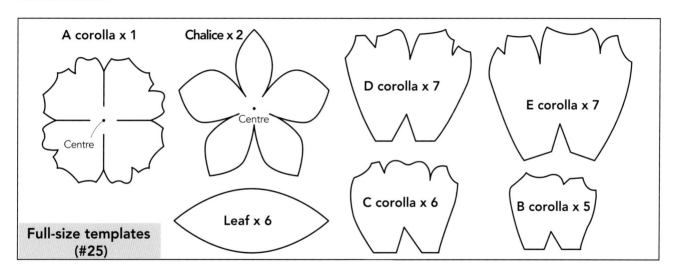

A corolla x 1

Chalice x 2
Centre

D corolla x 7

E corolla x 7

C corolla x 6

B corolla x 5

Leaf x 6

Centre

Full-size templates (#25)

Instructions

2. Periwinkle P. 6

Supplies
Felt
3 x 4 cm x 4 cm pieces violet (corollas)
6 x 2.5 cm x 4 cm pieces green (leaves)

Full-size templates below.

Other supplies
3 x 0.3 cm yellow beads (hearts)
15 x 0.2 cm white beads (corollas)
3 x 36 cm lengths of 0.37 mm steel wire (flowers)
6 x 18 cm lengths of 0.3 mm steel wire (leaves)
Green floral ribbon

1 Make the hearts.
A-2 (see p. 33)

Thread 1 bead onto 1 length of wire, then twist the wire 2 or 3 times at the base of the bead.

2 Make the flowers.
F-3 (see p. 35)

1

Sew the beads to the centre of the corolla, then tighten.

R (see p. 40)

2

Punch 1 hole in the centre of the corolla, then insert the heart wire. Glue together. Make 3 flowers.

3 Make the leaves.
E (see p. 35)

Punch 1 hole through the thickness of the felt, then insert and glue 1 length of wire. Make 6 leaves.

4 Assemble the flowers and the leaves.
S (see p. 40)

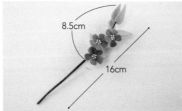

8.5cm

16cm

Join the flowers and the leaves by wrapping the floral ribbon around them. Cut the excess wire, then cover the ends with floral ribbon.

Full-size templates (#2)

Corolla x 3

Leaf x 6

Bead   Centre

Full-size templates (#3)

Heart x 5

Leaf x 5

Corolla x 5

Cut with notching scissors.

Full-size templates (#5)

Leaf x 12

3. French Marigold P. 6

a   b

Full-size templates p. 113

Supplies (from left to right: models a/b)
Felt
5 x 1.5 cm x 4.8 cm pieces light blue/purple (corollas)
5 x 3 cm x 3 cm pieces light yellow/yellow (hearts)
5 x 1.5 cm x 4 cm pieces dark green/green (leaves)

Other supplies (for each model)
5 x 36 cm lengths of 0.3 mm steel wire (flowers)
5 x 18 cm lengths of 0.3 mm steel wire (leaves)
Green floral ribbon

1 Make the hearts.
J (see p. 37)

Fold the heart in 2, then place the steel wire on the grooves of the folded component. Twist 2 or 3 times at the bottom.

2 Make the flowers.
G-1 (see p. 36)

_1_ Cut 1 long side of the corolla with the notching scissors. Notch the inner angles. Sew the unnotched side to form a ring.

_2_ Insert the heart wire in the centre of the corolla, then glue together. Make 5 flowers total.

3 Make the leaves.
E (see p. 35)

Punch 1 hole through the thickness of the felt, then insert and glue 1 length of wire. Make 5 leaves.

4 Assemble the flowers and the leaves.
S (see p. 40)

7cm   12cm

Join the flowers and the leaves by wrapping the floral ribbon around them. Cut excess wire and cover ends with floral ribbon.

---

5. Blue Daisy Bush P. 6

Supplies
Felt
3 x 2.5 cm x 3.5 cm pieces light blue (corollas)
12 x 2 cm x 3 cm pieces yellow-green (leaves)
Other supplies
3 x 36 cm lengths of 0.45 mm steel wire (flowers)
12 x 18 cm lengths of 0.3 mm steel wire (leaves)
3 x 0.8 cm yellow pompoms
Green floral ribbon

Full-size templates p. 44

1 Make the hearts.
K (see p. 37)

Make a circular support of 0.6 cm in diameter with 1 length of wire. Apply glue then glue to 1 pompom.

2 Make the flowers.
G-2 (see p. 36)

_1_ Fold the corolla in 2, then sew 1 long side. Notch over 1 cm, 0.3 cm apart. Stitch into the 1st stitch. Pull the thread to tighten.

_2_ Insert the heart wire in the centre of the corolla. Apply glue to the bottom of the heart.

_3_ Glue the heart to the corolla. Make 3 flowers.

3 Make the leaves.
E (see p. 35)

Punch 1 hole through the thickness of the felt, then insert and glue 1 length of wire. Make 12 leaves.

4 Assemble the flowers and the leaves.
S (see p. 40)

_1_ Join 1 flower and 4 leaves by wrapping the floral ribbon around them. Make 3 identical components.

_2_ 8cm   12cm

Join the 3 components from step 4-1 by wrapping the floral ribbon around them. Cut excess wire and cover ends with floral ribbon.

4. Swertia Pseudochinensis P. 6

Full-size templates on this page.

Supplies
Felt
5 x 3.5 cm x 3.5 cm pieces purple (corollas)
5 x 3.5 cm x 3.5 cm pieces yellow-green (chalices)
10 x 1.5 cm x 4 cm pieces yellow-green (leaves)
Other supplies
15 x 0.3 cm yellow-green beads (hearts)
5 x 36 cm lengths of 0.3 mm steel wire (flowers)
10 x 18 cm lengths of 0.3 mm steel wire (leaves)
Green floral ribbon

Full-size templates (#6)

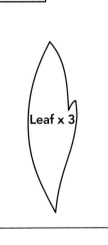

Corolla x 2

Centre

▨ = Apply glue.

Cut with notching scissors.

B heart x 1

Leaf x 3

① Make the hearts.
A-2 (see p. 33)

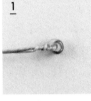

1 Thread 1 bead onto 1 length of wire, then twist 2 or 3 times at the base of the bead.

2 Thread 2 beads onto the 2 strands of wire.

② Make the flowers.
F-1 (see p. 35)

1 Sew the centre of the corolla. Pull the thread to tighten.

R (see p. 40)

2 Punch 1 hole in the centre of the corolla. Insert the heart wire. Apply glue to bottom of the heart.

3 Glue the heart and the corolla together.

③ Make the chalices.
R (see p. 40)

1 Punch 1 hole in the centre of the chalice. Insert the corolla wire. Apply glue to the bottom of the corolla.

2 Glue the corolla and the chalice together. Make 5 flowers.

④ Make the leaves.
E (see p. 35)

Punch 1 hole through the thickness of the felt, then insert and glue 1 length of wire. Make 10 leaves.

⑤ Assemble the flowers and the leaves.
S (see p. 40)

1 Join 1 flower and 2 leaves by wrapping the floral ribbon around them. Make 5 identical components.

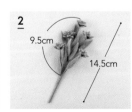

2 9.5cm 14.5cm
Join the components from step 5-1 by wrapping the floral ribbon around them. Cut excess wire and cover ends with floral ribbon.

Full-size templates (#4)

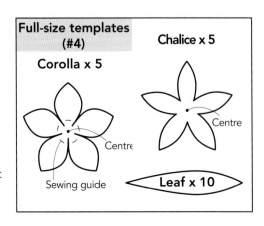

Corolla x 5

Sewing guide

Centre

Chalice x 5

Centre

Leaf x 10

6. African Daisy P. 6

Supplies

Felt

2 x 7 cm x 7 cm pieces purple (corollas)

1 x 1 cm x 7 cm piece dark blue (A heart)

1 x 1.2 cm x 3.9 cm piece yellow (B heart)

3 x 2 cm x 5.5 cm pieces yellow-green (leaves)

Other supplies

1 x 36 cm length of 0.55 mm steel wire (flower)

3 x 18 cm lengths of 0.3 mm steel wire (leaves)

Green floral ribbon

Full-size templates p. 46.

1 Make the heart.

H (see p. 36)

1

Roll up the A heart and sew bottom in a cross shape to secure.

G-1 (see p. 36)

2

Cut 1 side of the B heart with notching scissors. Notch the B heart.

3

Roll the B heart around the A heart. Sew bottom in a cross shape.

K (see p. 37)

4

Make a circular support of 0.8 cm in diameter with 1 length of wire.

5

Glue the heart from step 1-3 to the support.

2 Make the corollas.

N (see p. 38)

1

Apply glue as indicated by the template.

※The portions that need to be glued are greyed to help with comprehension.

2

Fold the petal in 2 and hold in place with a clamp. "

3

Fold all the petals in the same manner.

4

Once dry, remove clamps. Cut excess glue.

5

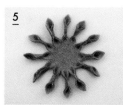

The corolla is finished. Make another corolla in the same manner.

3 Make the flower.

R (see p. 40)

1

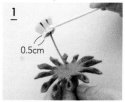

0.5cm

Punch 1 hole in the centre of the corolla. Insert the heart wire. Apply glue to the side and bottom of the heart.

2

Glue the corolla and the heart together.

3

Also glue the corolla to the side of the heart.

4

Glue 1 other corolla in the same manner, staggering the petals.

4 Make the leaves.

E (see p. 35)

Punch 1 hole through the thickness of the felt, then insert and glue 1 length of steel wire. Make 3 leaves.

5 Assemble the flowers and the leaves.

S (see p. 40)

9cm

14cm

Join the flowers and the leaves by wrapping the floral ribbon around them. Cut excess wire and cover ends with floral ribbon.

7. Anemone Pseudoaltaica P. 6

a   b

Full-size templates on this page.

Supplies (from left to right: models a/b)
Felt
4 x 3 cm x 3 cm pieces blue/purple (corollas)
5 x 4 cm x 4 cm pieces yellow-green/light green (leaves)
Other supplies (for each model)
2 x 0.3 cm yellow-green beads (hearts)
2 x 36 cm lengths of 0.3 mm steel wire (flowers)
5 x 18 cm lengths of 0.3 mm steel wire (leaves)
Green floral ribbon

---

1 Make the hearts.
A-2 (see p. 33)

Thread 1 bead onto 1 length of wire, then twist the wire 2 or 3 times close to the bead.

2 Make the flowers.
F-2 (see p. 35)

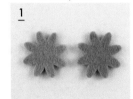

1

Cut 2 corollas.

2

Overlay the corollas, staggering the petals. Sew the centre.

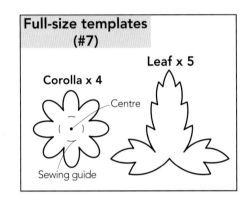

Full-size templates (#7)

Leaf x 5

Corolla x 4

Centre

Sewing guide

R (see p. 40)

3

Pull the thread to tighten.

4

Punch 1 hole in the centre of the corollas.

5

Insert the heart wire. Apply glue to the bottom of the bead.

6

Glue the heart. Make 2 flowers.

---

3 Make the leaves.   D (see p. 34)

1

Apply glue to the bottom of the leaf and glue 1 length of wire.

2

Fold the bottom of the leaf in 2 and hold in place with a clamp. Leave to dry. Make 5 leaves.

4 Assemble the flowers and the leaves.   S (see p. 40)

1

Make 1 component with 1 flower and 2 leaves, and 1 with 1 flower and 3 leaves. Wrap floral ribbon around them.

2

10.5cm   6.5cm

Join the 2 components from step 4-1 by wrapping the floral ribbon around them. Cut excess wire and cover ends with floral ribbon.

8. Baby Blue Eyes P. 6

Supplies

Felt

3 x 3 cm x 3 cm pieces light blue (corollas)

8 x 2.5 cm x 3.5 cm pieces yellow-green (leaves)

Other supplies

3 x 0.3 cm cream beads (hearts)

15 x 0.2 cm blue beads (corollas)

3 x 36 cm lengths of 0.37 mm steel wire (flowers)

8 x 18 cm lengths of 0.3 mm steel wire (leaves)

Green floral ribbon

Full-size templates on this page.

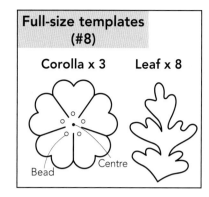

Full-size templates (#8)

Corolla x 3   Leaf x 8

Bead   Centre

① **Make the flowers.**

A-2 (see p. 33)

F-3 (see p. 35), R (see p. 40)

Make the heart with 1 cream bead and 2 lengths of wire. Sew 5 beads to the centre of the corolla, then tighten. Punch 1 hole in the centre of the corolla and insert the heart wire. Make 3 flowers.

② **Make the leaves.**

E (see p. 35)

Punch 1 hole through the thickness of the felt, then insert and glue 1 length of wire. Make 8 leaves.

③ **Assemble the flowers and the leaves.**

S (see p. 40)

1

Make 1 component with 1 flower and 2 leaves, and 2 more components with 1 flower and 3 leaves. Wrap floral ribbon around them.

2

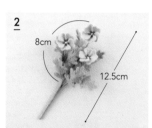

8cm

12.5cm

Join the components from step 3-1 by wrapping the floral ribbon around them. Cut excess wire and cover ends with floral ribbon.

---

9. Garden Heliotrope P. 6

Supplies

Felt

28 x 2 cm x 2 cm pieces violet (corollas)

5 x 2.5 cm x 4 cm pieces green (leaves)

Full-size templates below.

Other supplies

28 x 18 cm lengths of 0.3 mm steel wire (flowers)

5 x 18 cm lengths of 0.3 mm steel wire (leaves)

28 x 0.2 cm white beads (hearts)

Green floral ribbon

① **Make the flowers.**

A-1 (see p. 33),

F-1 (see p. 35), R (see p. 40)

Make the heart with 1 length of wire. Sew the centre of the corolla. Pull the thread to ruffle the corolla. Insert the heart wire in the centre of the corolla, then glue in place. Make 28 flowers.

② **Make the leaves.**

E (see p. 35)

Punch 1 hole through the thickness of the felt, then insert and glue 1 length of wire. Make 5 leaves.

③ **Assemble the flowers and the leaves.**

S (see p. 40)

7cm

13cm

Join the flowers and the leaves by wrapping the floral ribbon around them. Cut excess wire and cover ends with floral ribbon.

Full-size templates (#9)

Corolla x 28

Centre

Sewing guide

Leaf x 5

10. Dwarf Morning Glory P. 6

a   b

Full-size templates below.

Supplies (from left to right: models a/b)
Felt
3 x 3.5 cm x 3.5 cm pieces purple/light blue (corollas)
10 x 2 cm x 2.5 cm pieces yellow-green (leaves)
Other supplies (for each model)
3 x 0.3 cm yellow beads (hearts)
15 x 0.2 cm white beads (corollas)
3 x 36 cm lengths of 0.37 mm steel wire (flowers)
10 x 18 cm lengths of 0.3 mm steel wire (leaves)
Green floral ribbon

11cm
17.5cm

Make 3 flowers and 10 leaves following the instructions for model 2 on p. 44. Join the flowers and the leaves by wrapping floral ribbon around them. Cut excess wire and cover with floral ribbon.

---

11. Creeping Daisy P. 8

Supplies
Felt
2 x 5 cm × 5 cm pieces white (corollas)
3 x 3.5 cm × 5 cm pieces green (leaves)
Other supplies
1x 36 cm length of 0.55 mm steel wire (flower)
3 x 18 cm lengths of 0.3 mm steel wire (leaves)
1 x 1 cm yellow pompom
Green floral ribbon

Full-size templates below.

1 Make the heart.
K (see p. 37)

Make a circular support of 0.6 cm in diameter with 1 length of wire. Glue the pompom to the support.

2 Make the flower.
F-2 (see p. 35)

1

Overlay the 2 corollas, staggering the petals. Sew centre using the forward stitch.

3 Make the leaves.
E (see p. 35)

Punch a hole through the thickness of the felt, then insert and glue 1 length of wire. Make 3 leaves.

4 Assemble the flowers and the leaves.
S (see p. 40)

R (see p. 40)

2

Pull the thread to ruffle.

3

Punch 1 hole in the centre of the corollas, then insert the heart wire. Apply glue to the bottom of the heart.

4

Glue the heart to the corolla.

7cm
13.5cm

Join the flower and the leaves by wrapping the floral ribbon around them. Cut excess wire and cover ends with floral ribbon.

Full-size templates (#11)

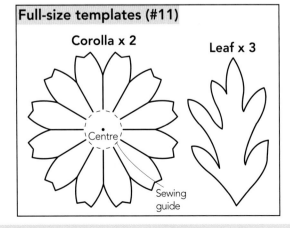

Corolla x 2

Leaf x 3

Centre

Sewing guide

Full-size templates (#10)

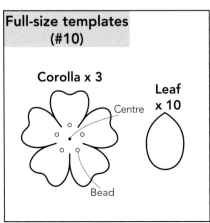

Corolla x 3

Centre

Leaf x 10

Bead

12. White Finch Lace P. 8

Supplies

Felt

5 x 3.5 cm x 3.5 cm pieces white (corollas)

1 x 3 cm x 3 cm piece white (A heart exterior)

1 x 3 cm x 3 cm piece white (A heart interior)

5 x 3 cm x 3 cm pieces white (B hearts)

2 x 4 cm x 5 cm pieces yellow-green (leaves)

Other supplies

1 x 36 cm length of 0.3 mm steel wire (A heart)

5 x 36 cm lengths of 0.3 mm steel wire (B hearts)

2 x 18 cm lengths of 0.3 mm steel wire (leaves)

Green floral ribbon

Full-size templates p. 83

---

1 Make the A heart.

J (see p. 37)   R (see p. 40)

1 Fold A heart interior component twice, then place 1 length of wire, folded in 2, in the groove. Twist the steel wire 2 or 3 times at the bottom of the heart.

2 Punch 1 hole in the centre of the A heart, then insert wire from step 1-1. Apply glue to the bottom of the A heart interior component.

Glue the A heart interior and exterior components together.

2 Make the B heart.

J (see p. 37)

Fold the B heart component twice, then place 1 length of wire, folded in 2, in the groove. Twist the steel wire 2 or 3 times at the bottom of the heart. Make 5 B hearts.

---

3 Make the flowers.

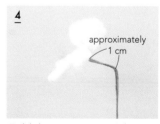

1 Apply glue to 2 consecutive petals.

2 Place the B heart between these petals.

3 Glue the B heart.

4 Fold the stem at a 90-degree angle, 1 cm from the corolla. Make 5 flowers.

approximately 1 cm

5 Join the 5 B hearts around the A heart.

6 Wrap the floral ribbon.

4 Make the leaves.

E (see p. 35)

Punch 1 hole through the thickness of the felt, then insert and glue 1 length of wire. Make 2 leaves.

5 Assemble the flowers and the leaves.

S (see p. 40)

7.5cm

17cm

Join the flower and the leaves by wrapping the floral ribbon around them. Cut excess wire and cover ends with floral ribbon.

13. Common Daisy P. 8

Supplies

Felt

1 x 4.5 cm x 6 cm piece white (corolla)

3 x 3 cm x 3 cm pieces yellow (heart)

3 x 4.5 cm x 6 cm pieces green (leaves)

Other supplies

1 x 36 cm length of 0.45 mm steel wire (flower)

3 x 18 cm lengths of 0.45 mm steel wire (leaves)

Green floral ribbon

Full-size templates on this page.

Full-size templates (#13)

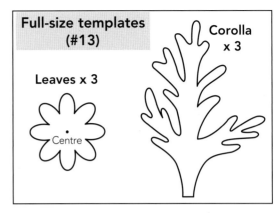

Leaves x 3
Centre

Corolla x 3

---

1 Make the heart.
J (see p. 37), R (see p. 40)

Fold 1 heart twice. Place 1 length of wire, folded in 2, in the groove. Twist the steel wire 2 or 3 times at the bottom of the heart. Punch 1 hole in the centre of the 2nd heart, then insert heart wire. Glue together.

Glue 3rd heart in the same manner, staggering the petals.

2 Make the flower.
G-2 (see p. 36)

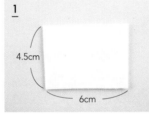

4.5cm

6cm

Prepare 1 white piece measuring 4.5 cm × 6 cm.

Fold in 2, then sew 1 long side. Notch over 1.8 cm, 0.3 cm apart. Stitch into 1st stitch to form a ring.

Insert heart wire in the centre of the corolla, then glue together.

3 Make the leaf.
E (see p. 35)

Punch 1 hole through the thickness of the felt, then insert and glue 1 length of wire. Make 3 leaves.

Full-size templates (#92)

Heart x 1

Leaf x 5

A petal x 4

B petal x 5

C petal x 6

Chalice x 1
Centre

---

4 Assemble the flowers and the leaves.
S (see p. 40)

9.5cm

18cm

Join the flower and the leaves by winding the floral ribbon around them. Cut excess wire and cover ends with floral ribbon.

14. Candytufts P. 8

Full-size templates on this page.

Supplies

Felt

1 x 3 cm x 3 cm piece yellow-green (interior heart)

1 x 3 cm x 3 cm piece light yellow (exterior heart)

8 x 3.5 cm x 3.5 cm pieces white (corollas)

5 x 1.5 cm x 4 cm pieces green (leaves)

Other supplies

8 x 0.3 cm orange beads (corollas)

1 x 36 cm length of 0.3 mm steel wire (heart)

8 x 36 cm lengths of 0.3 mm steel wire (corollas)

5 x 18 cm lengths of 0.3 mm steel wire (leaves)

Green floral ribbon

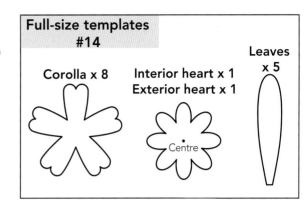

Full-size templates #14

Corolla x 8

Interior heart x 1
Exterior heart x 1

Centre

Leaves x 5

1 Make the heart.

J (see p. 37), R (see p. 40)

Fold interior heart twice, then place 1 length of wire, folded in 2, in the groove. Twist the steel wire 2 or 3 times at the bottom of the heart. Punch 1 hole in the centre of the exterior heart, then insert interior heart wire. Glue together.

2 Make the flower.

1

Apply glue to the bottom of 1 petal.

2

Glue consecutive petals.

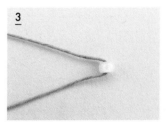

3

Thread 1 bead onto 1 length of wire, then fold in 2.

4

Place the wire over the 2 unglued petals from step 2-2.

5

Twist the wire 2 or 3 times at the bottom of the corolla.

6

Apply glue to the bead.

7

Glue 2 petals.

8

Fold wire at a 90-degree angle close to the corolla. Make 8 flowers.

9

Join the 8 flowers around the heart. Wrap floral ribbon around them.

3 Make the leaves.

E (see p. 35)

Punch a hole through the thickness of the felt, then insert and glue 1 length of wire. Make 5 leaves.

4 Assemble the flowers and the leaves.

S (see p. 40)

8cm

13cm

Join the flower and the leaves by wrapping the floral ribbon around them. Cut excess wire and cover ends with floral ribbon.

15. Feverfew - Chamomile P. 8

Supplies

Felt

6 x 3 cm x 3 cm pieces white (A corollas)
6 x 3.5 cm x 3.5 cm pieces white (B corollas)
3 x 3 cm x 3 cm pieces yellow (hearts)
6 x 3 cm x 4 cm pieces dark green (leaves)

Other supplies

3 x 36 cm lengths of 0.3 mm steel wire (hearts)
6 x 36 cm lengths of 0.3 mm steel wire (corollas)
6 x 18 cm lengths of 0.3 mm steel wire (leaves)
Green floral ribbon

Full-size templates below.

---

1 Make the hearts.

J (see p. 37)

Fold heart twice, then place 1 length of wire, folded in 2, in the groove. Twist the steel wire 2 or 3 times at the bottom of the heart.

2 Make the flowers.

J (see p. 37)

1

Fold the A corolla in 2. Place 1 length of wire, folded in 2, in the groove. Twist the steel wire 2 or 3 times at the bottom of the corolla. Make 2 components.

2

Join the heart and the 2 A corollas.

3

Twist the wires at the bottom of the A corollas.

R (see p. 40)

4

Punch 1 hole in the centre of the B corolla, then insert the wire from step 2-3. Apply glue to the bottom of the A corollas.

5

Glue the corollas together. Glue another B corolla, staggering the petals. Make 3 flowers.

3 Make the leaves.

E (see p. 35)

Punch 1 hole through the felt thickness of the felt, then insert and glue 1 length of wire. Make 6 leaves.

4 Assemble the flowers and the leaves.

S (see p. 40)

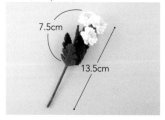

7.5cm

13.5cm

Join the flower and the leaves by wrapping the floral ribbon around them. Cut excess wire and cover ends with floral ribbon.

Full-size templates (#15)

A corolla x 6

B corolla x 6

Centre

Heart x 3

Leaf x 6

16. Dandelion P. 8

 a
 b

Full-size templates on this page.

Supplies

Felt
1 x 1.5 cm x 10 cm piece mustard (A corolla)
1 x 1.7 cm x 15.3 cm piece light yellow (B corolla)
1 x 3.5 cm x 3.5 cm piece yellow-green (A model, A chalice)
1 x 2 cm x 20 cm piece yellow (B model, C corolla)
1 x 4 cm x 4 cm piece yellow-green (B model, B chalice)
3 x 2.5 cm x 7.5 cm pieces yellow-green (leaves)

For each model
1 x 36 cm length of 0.55 mm steel wire (flower)
3 x 18 cm lengths of 0.45 mm steel wire (leaves)
Green floral ribbon

1 Make the flower.

G-1 (see p. 36)

1

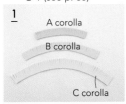
A corolla
B corolla
C corolla

Cut 1 long side of each corolla with the notching scissors (the C corolla is for model B).

H (see p. 36)

2

Roll up the A corolla, then sew the bottom in a cross shape.

3

Roll up the B corolla, then the C corolla (model B) around the small corolla. Sew the bottom in a cross shape.

2 Glue the chalice.

1

Make a circular support of 1.3 cm in diameter with 1 length of wire. Punch 1 hole in the centre of the chalice, then insert the wire. Apply glue.

K (see p. 37), R (see p. 40)

2

Glue the flower and chalice together.

3 Make the leaves.

E (see p. 35)

Punch 1 hole through the thickness of the felt, then insert and glue 1 length of wire. Make 3 leaves.

4 Assemble the flowers and the leaves.

S (see p. 40)

8.5cm
11.5cm

Join the flower and the leaves by wrapping the floral ribbon around them. Cut excess wire and cover ends with floral ribbon.

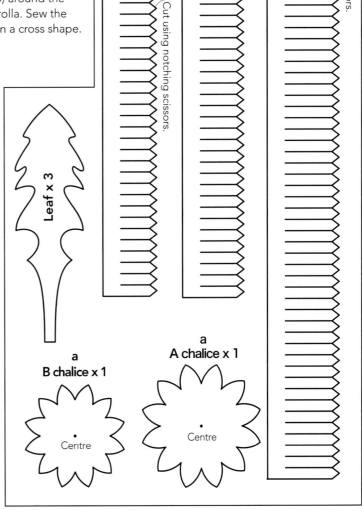

Full-size templates (#16)

a·b
B corolla x 1

Cut using notching scissors.

b
C corolla x 1

Cut using notching scissors.

a·b
A corolla x 1

Cut using notching scissors.

Leaf x 3

a
B chalice x 1
· Centre

a
A chalice x 1
· Centre

17. Feverfew P. 9

Supplies

Felt

6 x 4 cm x 4 cm pieces white (corollas)

9 x 3 cm x 3 cm pieces yellow (hearts)

3 x 3.5 cm x 4 cm pieces light green (leaves)

Other supplies

3 x 36 cm lengths of 0.3 mm steel wire (flowers)

3 x 18 cm lengths of 0.3 mm steel wire (leaves)

Green floral ribbon

Full-size templates on p. 57

1 Make the hearts.    J (see p. 37), R (see p. 40)

Fold the heart in 2, and place a length of wire, folded in 2, in the groove of the petals. Twist the wire 2 or 3 times at the bottom of the heart. Punch 1 hole in the centre of another heart, then insert the wire. Glue together.

Glue another heart, staggering the petals. Make 3 hearts.

2 Make the flowers.

R (see p. 40)

Punch 1 hole in the centre of a corolla, then insert the heart wire. Glue together.

Glue another corolla, staggering the petals. Make 3 flowers.

3 Make the leaves.

D (see p. 34)

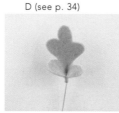

Apply glue to the bottom of a leaf, then glue a length of wire. Make 3 leaves.

4 Assemble the flowers and the leaves.

S (see p. 40)

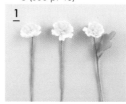

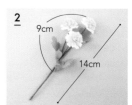

Wrap the floral ribbon around the stem of 2 flowers. Join the remaining flower and 1 leaf and wrap floral ribbon around them.

Join the flowers and the leaves by wrapping floral ribbon around them. Cut excess wire and cover ends with floral ribbon.

---

18. Jasmine P. 9

Supplies

Felt

6 x 3.5 cm x 3.5 cm pieces white (corollas)

3 x 3 cm x 5 cm pieces yellow-green (leaves)

Full-size templates below.

Other supplies

3 x 0.3 cm olive beads

3 x 36 cm lengths of 0.3 mm steel wire (flowers)

3 x 18 cm lengths of 0.3 mm steel wire (leaves)

Green floral ribbon

1 Make the flowers.

A-2 (see p. 33)

F-2 (see p. 35), R (see p. 40)

2 Make the leaves.

D (see p. 34)

3 Assemble the flowers and the leaves.

S (see p. 40)

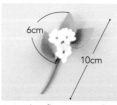

Make the heart with 2 strands of steel wire. Overlay 2 corollas, staggering the petals, then sew the centre. Pull the thread to tighten. Punch 1 hole in the centre of the corolla, then insert the heart wire and glue together. Make 3 flowers.

Apply glue to the bottom of a leaf, then glue 1 length of wire. Make 1 standalone leaf, and 2 leaves joined with floral ribbon.

Join the flowers and the leaves by wrapping floral ribbon around them. Cut excess wire and cover ends with floral ribbon.

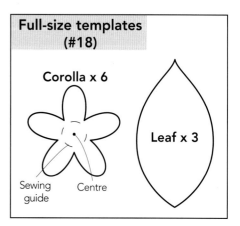

Full-size templates (#18)

Corolla x 6

Sewing guide   Centre

Leaf x 3

19. Silver Ragwort P. 9

Supplies

Felt

3 x 3 cm x 3 cm pieces yellow (bud hearts)
3 x 3 cm x 3 cm pieces yellow (bud corollas)
3 x 3 cm x 3 cm pieces yellow-green (bud chalices)
2 x 3 cm x 3 cm pieces yellow (flower hearts)
3 x 3.5 cm x 3.5 cm pieces light yellow (flower corollas)
3 x 4 cm x 5 cm pieces light green (leaves)

Other supplies

3 x 36 cm lengths of 0.3 mm steel wire (buds)
2 x 36 cm lengths of 0.3 mm steel wire (flowers)
3 x 18 cm lengths of 0.3 mm steel wire (leaves)
Green floral ribbon

Full-size templates below.

1 Make the buds. J (see p. 37), R (voir p. 40)

1

2

Fold the bud heart twice, then place a length of wire, folded in half, in the groove. Twist the wire 2 or 3 times at the bottom of the heart. Punch 1 hole in the centre of a bud corolla and insert the heart wire. Glue together.

Punch 1 hole in the centre of the bud chalice, insert the wire from step 1-1 and glue in place. Make 3 buds.

2 Make the flowers. J (see p. 37), R (see p. 40)

1

2

Fold the flower heart twice, then place a length of wire, folded in half, in the groove. Twist the wire 2 or 3 times at the bottom of the heart. Punch 1 hole in the centre of a flower corolla and insert the heart wire.

Glue together.

3 Make the leaves. D (see p. 34)

3

Glue another corolla, staggering the petals. Make 2 flowers.

Apply glue to the bottom of a leaf, then glue a length of wire. Make 3 leaves.

4 Assemble the flowers, the buds, and the leaves. S (see p. 40)

4.5cm

9cm

Join the flowers and the leaves by winding floral ribbon around them. Cut excess wire and cover ends with floral ribbon.

Full-size templates (#19)

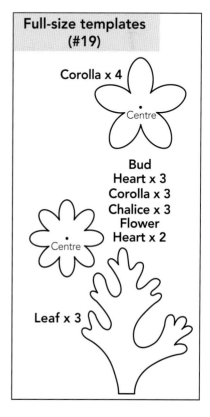

Corolla x 4

Centre

Bud
Heart x 3
Corolla x 3
Chalice x 3
Flower
Heart x 2

Centre

Leaf x 3

Full-size templates (#17)

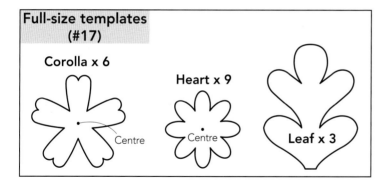

Corolla x 6

Heart x 9

Leaf x 3

Centre

Centre

20. Baby's Breath P. 9

Supplies
Felt
16 x 2 cm x 2 cm pieces white (corollas)
Other supplies
8 x 0.2 cm yellow beads (hearts)
8 x 36 cm lengths of 0.3 mm steel wire (flowers)
Green floral ribbon

Full-size templates on this page.

① Make the flowers.

A-2 (see p. 33), R (see p. 40)

② Assemble the flowers, the buds, and the leaves.

S (see p. 40)

A-2 (see p. 33), R (see p. 40)

1

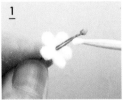

Make the heart with 2 lengths of wire. Punch 1 hole in the centre of a corolla and insert the heart wire. Glue together.

2

Glue another corolla, staggering the petals. Make 8 flowers.

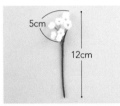

5cm
12cm

Join the flowers and the leaves by wrapping floral ribbon around them. Cut excess wire and cover ends with floral ribbon.

S (see p. 40)

---

21. Spanish Needles P. 9

Full-size templates on this page.

Supplies
Felt
6 x 3.5 cm x 3.5 cm pieces light yellow (corollas)
3 x 3 cm x 3 cm pieces yellow (hearts)
3 x 3.5 cm x 4 cm pieces light green (leaves)
Other supplies
3 x 36 cm lengths of 0.3 mm steel wire (flowers)
3 x 18 cm lengths of 0.3 mm steel wire (leaves)
Green floral ribbon

① Make the flowers.

J (see p. 37), R (see p. 40)

J (see p. 37), R (see p. 40)

② Make the leaves.

D (see p. 34)

D (see p. 34)

③ Assemble the flowers, the buds, and the leaves.

S (see p. 40)

S (see p. 40)

Fold the heart in 2, then place the steel wire on the groove. Twist 2 or 3 times at the bottom of the heart. Punch 1 hole in the centre of the corolla, then insert the heart wire. Glue 2 corollas together, staggering the petals. Make 3 flowers.

Apply glue to the bottom of a leaf, then glue 1 length of wire. Make 3 leaves.

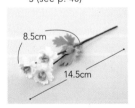

8.5cm
14.5cm

Wrap floral ribbon around each flower stem. Join the flowers and the leaves by wrapping floral ribbon around them. Cut excess wire and cover ends with floral ribbon.

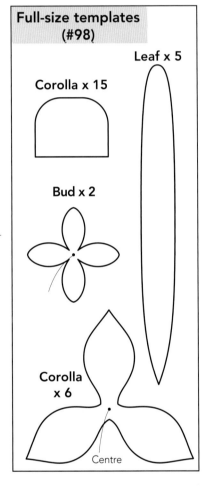

Full-size template (#20)

Corolla x 16

Centre

Full-size templates (#98)

Corolla x 15

Leaf x 5

Bud x 2

Corolla x 6

Centre

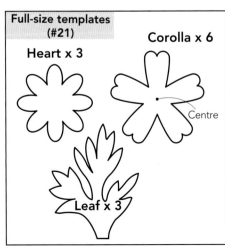

Full-size templates (#21)

Heart x 3

Corolla x 6

Centre

Leaf x 3

22. Mimosa P. 9

Supplies
12 x 0.8 cm yellow pompoms (flowers)
7 x 3 cm x 4 cm pieces yellow-green felt (leaves)
12 x 18 cm lengths of 0.3 mm steel wire (flowers)
7 x 18 cm lengths of 0.3 mm steel wire (leaves)
Green floral ribbon

Full-size templates on this page.

❶ Make the flowers.

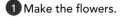

1

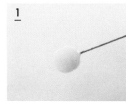

2

4.5cm

Apply glue to the end of a length of wire, then insert into a pompom. Make 12 components total.

Join the flowers and wrap floral ribbon around them.

❷ Make the leaf.

E (see p. 35)

1

2

x1   x2   x3

Punch 1 hole through the thickness of the felt, then insert 1 length of wire and glue in place. Make 7 leaves.

Join 3 leaves and wrap floral ribbon around them. Make 2 components with 3 leaves, and 1 with 1 leaf.

❸ Assemble the flowers and the leaves.

S (see p. 40)

7.5cm

11cm

Join the flowers and the leaves by winding floral ribbon around them. Cut excess wire and cover ends with floral ribbon.

Full-size template (#22)

Leaf x 7

Full-size template (#32)

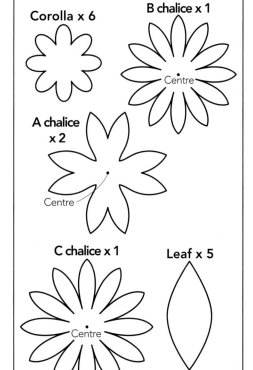

Corolla x 6

B chalice x 1

Centre

A chalice x 2

Centre

C chalice x 1

Leaf x 5

Centre

Full-size template (#24)

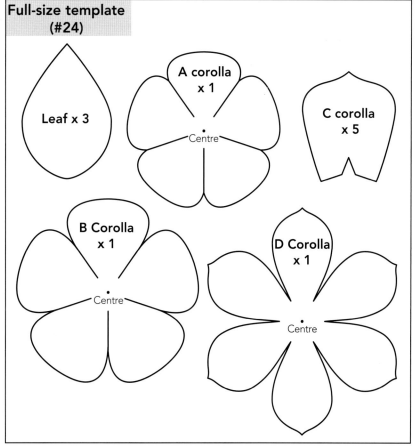

Leaf x 3

A corolla x 1

Centre

C corolla x 5

B Corolla x 1

Centre

D Corolla x 1

Centre

23. Clover P. 9

Supplies
Felt
3 x 3 cm x 3 cm pieces yellow (hearts)
3 x 3 cm x 3 cm pieces yellow (corollas)
10 x 2 cm x 2 cm pieces yellow-green (leaves)

Full-size templates on this page.

Other supplies
3 x 36 cm lengths of 0.3 mm steel wire (flowers)
10 x 18 cm lengths of 0.3 mm steel wire (leaves)
Green floral ribbon

① Make the hearts.
J (see p. 37)

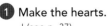

Fold the heart twice. Place 1 length of wire in the groove. Twist wire 2 or 3 times at bottom of component.

② Make the flowers.
R (see p. 40)

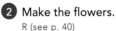

1. Punch 1 hole in the centre of the corolla, then insert the heart wire.

2. Glue together. Make 3 flowers.

Full-size template (#23)

Corolla x 3
Heart x 3

Centre

Leaf x 10

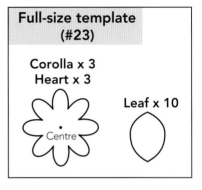

③ Make the leaves.
D (see p. 34)

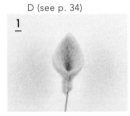

Apply glue to the bottom of the leaf, then place 1 length of wire on it. Pinch the bottom of the leaf to glue together.

Apply glue to 1 leaf and glue it to another leaf.

Hold the 2 leaves together with a clamp and leave to dry.

Full-size template (#101)

Pistil x 1

Centre

Leaf x 5

Sewing guide

B petal x 3

A petal x 3

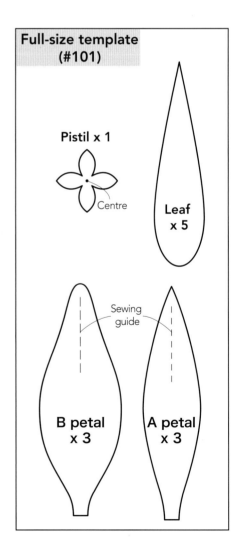

Make 2 identical components.

Glue the 3rd leaf following steps 3-1 to 3. Make 2 identical components.

④ Assemble the flowers and the leaves.
S (see p. 40)

5cm
10cm

Join the flowers and the leaves by winding floral ribbon around them. Cut excess wire and cover ends with floral ribbon.

24. Gardenia Taitensis P. 10

Supplies
Felt
1 x 5 cm x 5 cm piece white (A corolla)
1 x 6 cm x 6 cm piece white (B corolla)
5 x 4 cm x 4 cm pieces white (C corolla)
1 x 7 cm x 7 cm piece white (D corolla)
3 x 3.5 cm x 5 cm pieces dark green (leaves)

Other supplies
1 x 1 cm beige wooden bead
1 x 36 cm length of 0.8 mm steel wire (flower)
3 x 18 cm lengths of 0.37 mm steel wire (leaves)
Green floral ribbon

Full-size templates on p. 59

1 Make the flower.

N (see p. 38)

1

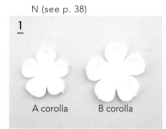

A corolla   B corolla

Apply glue to the top of the petals and pinch. Make the A and the B corollas.

B-3 (see p. 33)

2

Thread the wooden bead onto 1 length of steel wire, then twist the wire 2 or 3 times close to the bead.

C-2 (see p. 34)

3

Punch 1 hole in the centre of the A corolla, then insert the wire from step 1-2. Apply glue to the bead and glue the   corolla to hide the bead.

R (see p. 40)

4

Punch 1 hole in the centre of the B corolla, then insert the wire from step 1-3. Apply glue to bottom of the A corolla and glue together.

P (see p. 39)

5

Make a cup with the C corolla components.

6

Insert the wire from step 1-4 in the C corolla. Apply glue to the B corolla.

7

Glue the corollas.

P (see p. 40)

8

Punch 1 hole in the centre of the D corolla, then insert the wire from step 1-7. Apply glue to the C corolla.

9

Glue the corollas.

2 Make the leaves.
E (see p. 35)

Punch 1 hole through the thickness of the felt, then insert and glue 1 length of wire. Make 3 leaves.

3 Assemble the flowers and the leaves.
S (see p. 40)

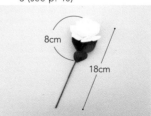

8cm

18cm

Join the flowers and the leaves by wrapping floral ribbon around them. Cut excess wire and cover ends with floral ribbon.

25. Chinese Peony P. 10

Full-size templates on p. 43

Supplies

Felt

1 x 4.5 cm x 4.5 cm piece pink (A corolla)
5 x 3 cm x 3.5 cm pieces pink (B corolla)
6 x 3.5 cm x 4 cm pieces pink (C corolla)
7 x 4 cm x 4.5 cm pieces light pink (D corolla)
7 x 4.5 cm x 5 cm pieces light pink (E corolla)
2 x 5 cm x 5 cm pieces green (chalices)
6 x 2.5 cm x 5 cm pieces green (leaves)

Other supplies

1 x 0.6 cm beige wooden bead (heart)
1 x 36 cm length of 0.8 mm steel wire (flower)
6 x 18 cm lengths of 0.45 mm steel wire (leaves)
Green floral ribbon

① Make the flower.

B-3 (see p. 33)

1

Thread the wooden bead onto 1 length of steel wire, then twist the wire 2 or 3 times close to the bead.

C-1 (see p. 34)

2

Punch 1 hole in the centre of the A corolla, then insert wire from step 1-1. Apply glue to the bead.

3

Apply glue to the petals and glue them around the bead.

P (see p. 39)

4

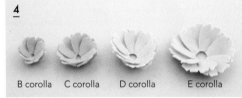

B corolla   C corolla   D corolla   E corolla

Sew the 5 petals of the B corolla, the 6 petals of the C corolla and the 7 petals of the D and E corollas to create a cup.

5

Insert the wire from step 1-3 in the centre of the B corolla. Apply glue to the bottom of the A corolla.

6

Glue corollas together.

7

Insert the wire from step 1-6 in the centre of the C corolla. Glue together.

8

Insert the wire from step 1-7 in the centre of the D corolla. Glue together.

9

Insert the wire from step 1-8 in the centre of the E corolla. Glue together.

② Glue the chalice.

R (see p. 40)

1

Punch 1 hole in the centre of the chalice and insert the flower wire. Apply glue to the chalice.

2

Glue together.

3

Glue another chalice, staggering the petals.

③ Make the leaves.

E (see p. 35)

Punch 1 hole through the thickness of the felt, then insert and glue 1 length of wire. Make 6 leaves. Join 3 leaves by wrapping floral ribbon around them. Make 2 identical components.

④ Assemble the flowers and the leaves.

S (see p. 40)

8.5cm

19cm

Join the flowers and the leaves by wrapping floral ribbon around them. Cut excess wire and cover ends with floral ribbon.

26. Peony P. 10

Full-size templates on p. 77

Supplies

Felt

13 x 4 cm x 5 cm pieces red (A and B corollas)

8 x 4.5 cm x 5.5 cm pieces flat red (C corolla)

1 x 5 cm x 5 cm piece light maroon (A heart)

1 x 1.5 cm x 9 cm piece yellow (B heart)

2 x 5 cm x 5 cm pieces green (chalice)

2 x 3 cm x 5 cm pieces green (A leaves)

2 x 5 cm x 5 cm pieces green (B leaves)

Other supplies

1 x 1 cm beige wooden bead (heart)

1 x 36 cm length of 0.8 mm steel wire (flower)

4 x 18 cm lengths of 0.45 mm steel wire (leaves)

Green floral ribbon

❶ Make the heart.

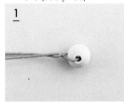

B-3 (see p. 33)

1 Thread the wooden bead onto 1 length of steel wire, then twist the wire 2 or 3 times close to the bead.

C-1 (see p. 34)

2 Punch 1 hole in the centre of the A corolla, then insert wire from step 1-1. Glue together.

❷ Make the flower.

G-1 (see p. 36)

3 Notch the B heart over 1 cm, 0.3 cm apart.

4 Apply glue to the unnotched side and roll the B heart around the A heart twice.

M (see p. 38)

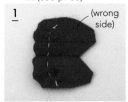

1 (wrong side) Sew the petals of the A to C corollas. Pull the thread to ruffle.

P (see p. 39)

2 A corolla (5 petals) B corolla (8 petals) B corolla (8 petals)

Assemble the petals as above to form a cup and make the A to C corollas.

3 0.5cm

Insert the heart wire in the centre of the A corolla. Apply glue to the side and bottom of the heart.

4 Glue together.

5 Insert the wire from step 2-4 in the centre of the B corolla, then glue together.

6 Insert the wire from step 2-5 in the centre of the C corolla, then glue together.

❸ Glue the chalices.

R (see p. 40)

Punch 1 hole in the centre of the chalice, then insert the flower wire and glue together. Glue another chalice, staggering the petals.

❹ Make the leaves.

E (see p. 35)

Punch 1 hole through the thickness of the felt, then insert and glue 1 length of wire. Make 1 component with 1 B leaf and 1 component with 2 A leaves and 1 B leaf.

❺ Assemble the flowers and the leaves.

S (see p. 35)

8cm

19cm

Join the flowers and the leaves by wrapping floral ribbon around them. Cut excess wire and cover ends with floral ribbon.

27. Buttercup P. 10

Full-size templates on
p. 84

Supplies
Felt
1 x 5 cm x 5 cm piece light maroon (heart)
4 x 3.5 cm x 3.5 cm pieces light maroon (A corolla)
5 x 4 cm x 4 cm pieces light orange (B corolla)
5 x 4.5 cm x 4.5 cm pieces light orange (C corolla)
13 x 5.5 cm x 5.5 cm pieces light orange (D and E corollas)
2 x 5 cm x 5 cm pieces light green (chalices)
3 x 6 cm x 6 cm pieces light green (leaves)

Other supplies
1 x 1 cm beige wooden bead (heart)
1 x 36 cm length of 0.8 mm steel wire (flower)
3 x 18 cm lengths of 0.45 mm steel wire (leaves)
Green floral ribbon

1 Make the heart.

B-3 (see p. 33), C-1 (see p. 34)

Thread the wooden
bead onto 1 length of
steel wire, then twist the
wire 2 or 3 times close
to the bead. Insert the
wire in the centre of the
heart and glue together.

2 Make the flower.   P (see p. 39)

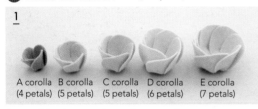

1
A corolla   B corolla   C corolla   D corolla   E corolla
(4 petals) (5 petals) (5 petals) (6 petals) (7 petals)

Assemble the petals as above to form a cup to
make the A to E corollas.

2

Insert the heart wire in the A
corolla. Glue together.

3

Insert the wire from step 2-2 in
the B corolla. Glue together.

3 Glue the chalices.

R (see p. 40)

4 Make the leaves.

E (see p. 35)

**5 Assemble the flowers and
the leaves.**

S (see p. 40)

4

Glue corollas C to E in the
same manner.

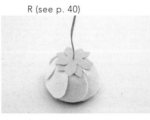

Punch 1 hole in the centre of
the chalice, then insert the
flower wire and glue together.
Glue another chalice,
staggering the petals.

Punch 1 hole through the
thickness of the felt, then
insert and glue 1 length of
wire. Make 3 leaves.

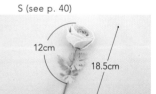

12cm

18.5cm

Join the flowers and the
leaves by wrapping floral
ribbon around them. Cut
excess wire and cover ends
with floral ribbon.

**Full-size templates
(#28)**

A petal x 6

B petal x 6

Sewing
guide

Leaf
x 5

Chalice x 1

Centre

28. Prairie Gentian P. 10

Full-size templates
on p. 64

Supplies
Felt
6 x 3.5 cm x 5 cm pieces purple (A petals)
6 x 4 cm x 5 cm pieces purple (B petals)
1 x 5 cm x 5 cm piece green (chalice)
5 x 2 cm x 5 cm pieces green (leaves)
Other supplies
12 x 18 cm lengths of 0.3 mm steel wire (petals)
5 x 18 cm lengths of 0.3 mm steel wire (pistils)
No. 25 yellow embroidery thread (pistils)
Green floral ribbon

1 Make the pistils.
Q (see p. 40)

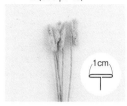

1cm

Cut embroidery thread and glue onto the 5 lengths of steel wire after folding these in a "T" shape. Make 5 pistils and join them together by wrapping floral ribbon around them.

2 Make the petals.
E (see p. 35)

1

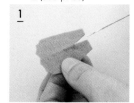

Punch 1 hole through the thickness of the felt, then insert and glue 1 length of wire.

3 Make the flower.
P (see p. 39)

2

Make 6 A petals and 6 B petals.

1

Overlay the sides of the B petals and make 1 stitch at the bottom.

2

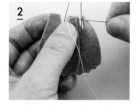

Pull the thread and sew in the same place.

3

Pull the thread.

4

As per steps 3-1 to 3, assemble the 6 petals to form a cup.

5 large corolla / small corolla

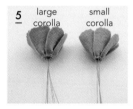

Assemble the A petals in the same manner.

6

Overlay the A petals and sew along the sewing guide.

7

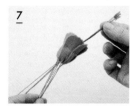

Insert the heart wire in the centre of the small corolla.

8

Wrap floral ribbon over 2 cm.

9

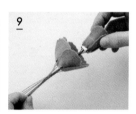

Apply glue to the bottom of the small corolla, then insert the wire into the large corolla.

10

Glue together.

4 Glue the chalice.
R (see p. 40)

1

Punch 1 hole in the centre of the chalice, then insert the flower wire. Apply glue to the chalice.

2

Glue together.

5 Make the leaves.
E (see p. 35)

Punch 1 hole through the thickness of the felt, then insert and glue 1 length of wire. Make 5 leaves.

6 Assemble the flowers and the leaves.
S (see p. 40)

11.5cm
18cm

Join the flowers and the leaves by wrapping floral ribbon around them. Cut excess wire and cover ends with floral ribbon.

29. Carnation P. 29

a   c

b   d

Full-size templates on p. 79

Supplies (from left to right: models a/b/d)
Felt
5 x /1 x /3 x 4.5 cm x 4.5 cm pieces dark red (petals)
1 x 3 cm x 4.5 cm piece dark green (A chalice)
1 x 3 cm x 3 cm piece dark green (B chalice)
4 x 1.5 cm x 4 cm pieces dark green (leaves)
c
5 x 4.5 cm x 4.5 cm pieces light pink (petals)
1 x 3 cm x 4.5 cm piece yellow-green (A chalice)
1 x 3 cm x 3 cm piece green (B chalice)
4 x 1.5 cm x 4 cm pieces green (leaves)
Other supplies (for each model)
1 x 0.8 cm x 1 cm beige wooden bead
From left to right: models a/b/c/d
5 x /1 x /5 x / 3 x 36 cm lengths of 0.3 mm steel wire (petals)
4 x 18 cm lengths of 0.3 mm steel wire (leaves)
Green floral ribbon

① Make the flower.
J (see p. 37)

1

Fold petal twice.

2

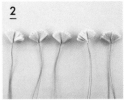

Place 1 length of wire, folded in 2, on the groove. Twist the wire 2 or 3 times at the bottom of the petal. Make 5 components (a, c). Make 1 component (b). Make 3 components (d).

3

Assemble the components from step 1-2.

4

Twist the wires 2 or 3 times at the bottom of the petals.

② Glue the chalices.

1

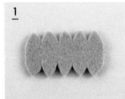

Cut A chalice as per the template.

2

Fold in 2.

3   I (see p. 37)

Sew the side using the overlock stitch. Make 2 or 3 stitches at the ends.

4

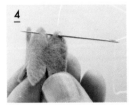

Insert needle through the peaks.

5

Pull thread to tighten. Do not cut the thread.

6

Thread bead onto flower wire. Apply glue to the bottom of the flower.

7

Pull the chalice onto the wire, tightened edge toward the bottom.

8

Apply glue to the bead.

9

Glue the chalice. Pull the thread. Secure with a knot.

10   R (see p. 40)

Punch 1 hole in the centre of the B chalice, then insert the wire from step 2-9. Apply glue to the B chalice.

11

Glue in place.

③ Make the leaves.
E (see p. 35)

Punch 1 hole through the thickness of the felt, then insert and glue 1 length of wire. Make 4 leaves.

④ Assemble the flowers and the leaves.
S (see p. 40)

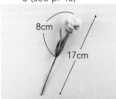

8cm

17cm

Join the flowers and the leaves by wrapping floral ribbon around them. Cut excess wire and cover ends with floral ribbon.

30. Gerbera P. 13

 a    b

Supplies (from left to right: models a/b)

Felt

1 x 0.5 cm x 5 cm piece green/maroon (A heart)

1 x 1 cm x 7.5 cm piece maroon/yellow (B heart)

1 x 1.2 cm x 16.2 cm piece very dark orange/coral (C heart)

3 x 8 cm x 8 cm pieces dark orange/light orange (A corollas)

2 x 8 cm x 8 cm pieces dark orange/light orange (B corollas)

1 x 4.5 cm x 4.5 cm piece green/yellow-green (chalice)

3 x 2 cm x 5.5 cm pieces green/yellow-green (leaves)

Other supplies (for each model)

1 x 36 cm length of 0.8 mm steel wire (flower)

3 x 18 cm lengths of 0.3 mm steel wire (leaves)

Green floral ribbon

Full-size templates on p. 73

1 Make the heart.

H (see p. 36)

1

Roll up the A heart and sew the bottom in a cross shape to secure.

G-1 (see p. 36)

2

Notch the long side of the B heart over 0.5 cm, 0.3 cm apart.

3

Roll the B heart around the A heart, then sew bottom in a cross shape to secure.

4

Cut 1 long side of the C heart with the notching scissors, then roll it up around the B heart and sew the bottom in a cross shape to secure.

2 Make the flower.

1

0.5cm

Apply glue to the bottom and side of the heart.

2

Glue the heart to the centre of the A corolla.

3

Lift the petals and glue them to the heart.

4

Glue 2 more A corollas, staggering the petals.

5

Apply glue to the bottom and side of the A corolla, then glue to the centre of the B corolla.

6

Glue 1 more B corolla, staggering the petals.

3 Glue the chalice.

K (see p. 37), R (see p. 40)

1

Make a circular support of 1.5 cm in diameter with 1 length of wire. Punch 1 hole in the centre of the chalice, then insert the wire.

2

Apply glue to the chalice, then glue to the bottom of the flower.

4 Make the leaves.

E (see p. 35)

Punch 1 hole through the thickness of the felt, then insert and glue 1 length of wire. Make 3 leaves.

5 Assemble the flowers and the leaves.

S (see p. 40)

11.5cm

17.5cm

Join the flowers and the leaves by wrapping floral ribbon around them. Cut excess wire and cover ends with floral ribbon.

31. Red Daisy P. 13

a   b

Full-size templates on this page.

Supplies (from left to right: models a/b)
Felt
1 x 1 cm x 4.5 cm piece yellow/light yellow (heart)
1 x 1.5 cm x 6 cm piece dark red/dark pink (A corolla)
1 x 1.5 cm x 14.7 cm piece red/pink (B corolla)
1 x 3 cm x 3 cm piece dark green/green (chalice)
3 x 2.5 cm x 4.5 cm pieces dark green/green (leaves)

Other supplies (for each model)
1 x 36 cm length of 0.55 mm steel wire (flower)
3 x 18 cm lengths of 0.3 mm steel wire (leaves)
Green floral ribbon

---

1 Make the heart.
G-1 (see p. 36)

1

Notch the long side of the heart over 0.5 cm, 0.3 cm apart.

2

Roll up the heart and sew bottom in a cross shape to secure.

H (see p. 36)

2

Roll the A corolla around the heart and sew bottom in a cross shape to secure.

3

Roll the B corolla around the A corolla and sew bottom in a cross shape to secure.

2 Make the flower.
G-1 (see p. 36)

1

A

B

Cut the long sides of the A and B corollas using notching scissors.

3 Glue the chalice.
K (see p. 37), R (see p. 40)

1

Make a circular support of 1.2 cm in diameter with 1 length of wire. Punch 1 hole in the centre of the chalice, then insert the wire.

2

Apply glue to the chalice, then glue to the bottom of the flower.

4 Make the leaves.
E (see p. 35)

Punch 1 hole through the thickness of the felt, then insert and glue 1 length of wire. Make 3 leaves.

5 Assemble the flowers and the leaves.
S (see p. 40)

7.5cm

11cm

Join the flowers and the leaves by wrapping floral ribbon around them. Cut excess wire and cover ends with floral ribbon.

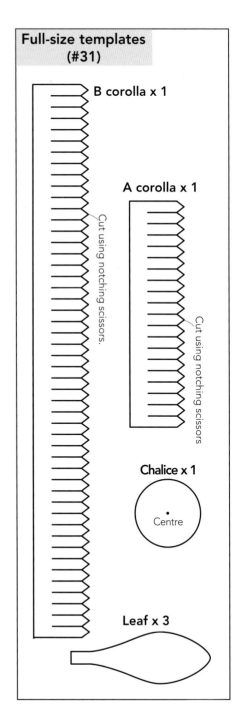

Full-size templates (#31)

B corolla x 1

Cut using notching scissors.

A corolla x 1

Cut using notching scissors

Chalice x 1

Centre

Leaf x 3

32. Safflower P. 13

Full-size templates on p. 59

Supplies
Felt
6 x 3 cm x 3 cm pieces orange (petals)
2 x 4 cm x 4 cm pieces yellow-green (A chalices)
1 x 4 cm x 4 cm piece green (B chalice)
1 x 4.5 cm x 4.5 cm piece green (C chalice)
5 x 2 cm x 4 cm pieces green (leaves)

Other supplies
1 x 0.8 cm x 1 cm beige wooden bead (chalice)
6 x 36 cm length of 0.3 mm steel wire (flower)
5 x 18 cm lengths of 0.3 mm steel wire (leaves)
Green floral ribbon

---

1 Make the flower.

J (see p. 37)

Fold petal twice, then place 1 length of wire, folded in two, in the groove. Twist the wire 2 or 3 times at the base of the petal. Make 6 components. Assemble them and twist the wires at the bottom of the petals.

2 Glue the chalices.

C-1 (see p. 34)

1

Thread the bead onto the flower wire. Punch 1 hole in the centre of the A chalice, then insert the wire.

2

Apply glue to the A chalice.

3

Glue together. Insert the wire in another A chalice and apply glue.

4

Glue together.

5

Apply glue to the bottom of the flower.

6

Glue the flower and chalice together.

R (see p. 40)

7

Punch 1 hole in the centre of the B chalice, then insert the 2-6 wire. Glue together.

8

Glue the C chalice in the same manner.

3 Make the leaves.

D (see p. 34)

Apply glue to the bottom of the leaf and glue 1 length of wire to it. Make 5 leaves.

4 Assemble the flowers and the leaves.

S (see p. 40)

1

Join the flowers and the leaves by wrapping floral ribbon around them.

2

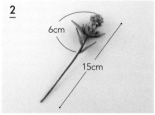

6cm
15cm

Cut excess wire and cover ends with floral ribbon.

33. Cosmos P. 13

a   b

Full-size templates on this page.

Supplies (from left to right: models a/b)
Felt
1 x 3 cm x 3 cm piece yellow (heart)
1 x 6 cm x 6 cm piece red/pink (corolla)
1 x 4.5 cm x 4.5 cm piece red/pink (bud)
1 x 3 cm x 3 cm piece light green/green (chalice)
2 x 4 cm x 4.5 cm pieces light green/green (leaves)

Other supplies (for each model)
1 x 36 cm length of 0.55 mm steel wire (flower)
1 x 36 cm length of 0.55 mm steel wire (bud)
2 x 18 cm lengths of 0.55 mm steel wire (leaves)
1 x 0.3 cm purple bead (bud)
1 x 0.8 cm beige wooden bead (bud)
Green floral ribbon

1 Make the heart.
J (see p. 37)

Fold the heart twice, then attach 1 length of wire, folded in 2. Twist the wire 2 or 3 times at the base of the heart.

2 Make the flower.
F-1 (see p. 35)

<u>1</u>

Sew the centre of the corolla. Pull thread to ruffle.

R (see p. 40)

<u>2</u>

Punch 1 hole in the centre of the corolla, then insert the heart wire and glue in place.

3 Make the bud.
B-1 (see p. 33)

<u>1</u>

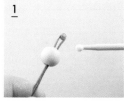

Thread the purple bead onto 1 length of wire, then fold wire in 2. Thread the wooden bead over the 2 strands of wire and glue in place.

C-3 (see p. 34)

<u>2</u>

Punch 1 hole in the centre of the bud, then insert the wire from step 3-1 and glue in place.

R (see p. 40)

<u>3</u>

Punch 1 hole in the centre of the chalice, then insert the wire from step 3-2 and glue in place.

4 Make the leaves.
E (see p. 35)

Punch 1 hole through the thickness of the felt and insert 1 length of wire. Glue in place. Make 2 leaves.

5 Assemble the flower, bud, and leaves.
S (see p. 40)

<u>1</u>

Wrap floral ribbon around the stems of the flower and of the bud.

<u>2</u>

9cm   17cm

Join the flower, bud, and leaves by wrapping floral ribbon around them. Cut excess wire and cover ends with floral ribbon.

Full-size templates (#33)

Bud corolla x 1

Centre

Bud chalice x 1   Heart x 1

Centre

Corolla x 1

Centre

Sewing guide

Leaf x 2

34. Flower of Bristol P. 13

Full-size templates on this page.

Supplies

Felt

7 x 3 cm x 3 cm pieces dark orange (corollas)

4 x 2.5 cm x 5 cm pieces green (leaves)

Other supplies

7 x 0.3 cm olive beads (hearts)

7 x 36 cm lengths of 0.3 mm steel wire (flowers)

4 x 18 cm lengths of 0.3 mm steel wire (leaves)

Green floral ribbon

---

1 Make the flower.

A-2 (see p. 33),
F-1 (see p. 35), R (see p. 40)

Thread the bead onto 1 length of wire and make the heart with 2 strands of wire. Sew the centre of the corolla and ruffle. Punch 1 hole in the centre and insert the heart wire. Glue together. Make 7 flowers.

2 Make the leaves.

E (see p. 35)

Punch 1 hole through the thickness of the felt and insert 1 length of wire. Glue in place. Make 4 leaves.

3 Assemble the flower and the leaves.

S (see p. 40)

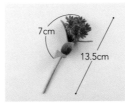

7cm
13.5cm

Join the flower and the leaves by wrapping floral ribbon around them. Cut excess wire and cover ends with floral ribbon.

Full-size templates (#34)

Corolla x 7

Centre

Sewing guide

Leaf x 4

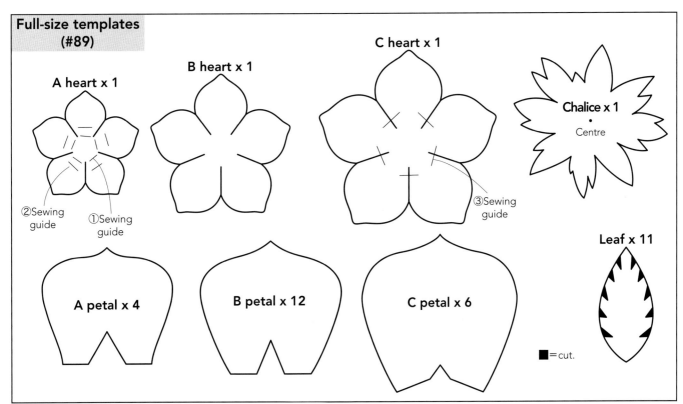

Full-size templates (#89)

A heart x 1

②Sewing guide   ①Sewing guide

B heart x 1

C heart x 1

③Sewing guide

Chalice x 1

Centre

A petal x 4

B petal x 12

C petal x 6

■ = cut.

Leaf x 11

35. Vervain P. 13

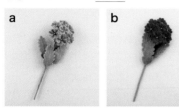

a   b

Full-size templates on p. 73.

Supplies
Felt (from left to right: models a/b)
7 x 3.5 cm x 3.5 cm pieces pink/red (corollas)
3 x 3 cm x 5.5 cm pieces yellow-green/green (leaves)

Other supplies (for each model)
7 x 36 cm lengths of 0.3 mm steel wire (flowers)
3 x 18 cm lengths of 0.3 mm steel wire (leaves)
7 x 0.3 cm yellow-green beads (hearts)
Green floral ribbon

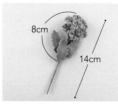

8cm

14cm

Make 7 flowers and 3 leaves as per model 34 on p. 71. Assemble the flowers and the leaves by wrapping floral ribbon around them. Cut excess wire and cover ends with floral ribbon.

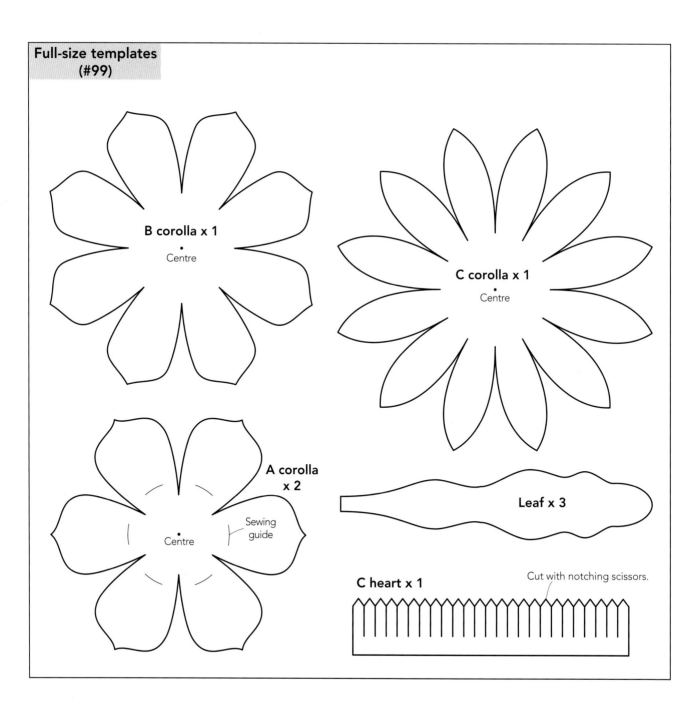

Full-size templates (#99)

B corolla x 1
Centre

C corolla x 1
Centre

A corolla x 2
Centre
Sewing guide

Leaf x 3

C heart x 1

Cut with notching scissors.

36. Egyptian Starcluster P. 13

a

b

Full-size templates on this page.

Supplies

Felt (from left to right: models a/b)

16 x 2 cm x 2 cm pieces light pink/red (corollas)

4 x 2 cm x 4.5 cm pieces green/dark green (leaves)

Other supplies (for each model)

16 x 0.2 cm white beads (hearts)

16 x 36 cm lengths of 0.3 mm steel wire (flowers)

4 x 18 cm lengths of 0.3 mm steel wire (leaves)

Green floral ribbon

1 Make the flower.

A-2 (see p. 33),
R (see p. 40)

Make 16 flowers as per model 39 on p. 74. Join in a half-globe shape, them wrap with floral ribbon.

2 Make the leaves.

D (see p. 34)

Apply glue to the bottom of a leaf and glue 1 length of wire. Make 4 leaves, then assemble them with floral ribbon.

3 Assemble the flower and the leaves.

S (see p. 40)

4.5cm
9cm

Join the flowers and the leaves by wrapping floral ribbon around them. Cut excess wire and cover ends with floral ribbon.

Full-size templates (#36)

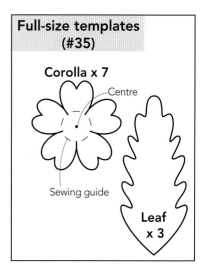

Corolla x 16

Centre

Leaf x 4

Full-size templates (#35)

Corolla x 7

Centre

Sewing guide

Leaf x 3

Full-size templates # 30

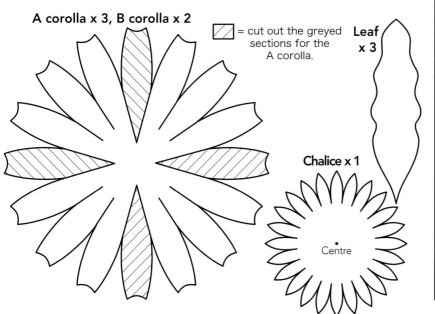

A corolla x 3, B corolla x 2

= cut out the greyed sections for the A corolla.

Leaf x 3

Chalice x 1

Centre

C heart x 1

Cut with notching scissors.

37. Chinese Ixora P. 13

a   b

Full-size templates below.

Supplies
Felt (from left to right: models a/b)

26 x 3 cm x 3 cm pieces dark orange/light orange (corollas)

5 x 2.5 cm x 4.5 cm pieces dark green/very dark green (leaves)

Other supplies (for each model)
26 x 0.2 cm light orange/purple beads (hearts)

26 x 36 cm lengths of 0.3 mm steel wire (flowers)

5 x 18 cm lengths of 0.3 mm steel wire (leaves)

Green floral ribbon

5cm

11cm

Make 26 flowers and 5 leaves as per model 34 on p. 71. Assemble the flowers and the leaves by wrapping floral " ribbon around them. Cut excess wire and cover ends with floral ribbon.

---

39. West Indian lantana P. 13

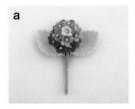

a   b

Supplies
Felt (from left to right: models a/b)

1 x 2 cm x 2 cm piece yellow (A corolla)

6 x 2 cm x 2 cm pieces orange/light pink (B corolla)

9 x 2 cm x 2 cm pieces dark orange/pink (C corolla)

2 x 4 cm x 5.5 cm pieces yellow-green/green (leaves)

Other supplies (for each model)
16 x 0.3 cm orange beads (hearts)

16 x 36 cm lengths of 0.3 mm steel wire (flowers)

2 x 18 cm lengths of 0.3 mm steel wire (leaves)

Green floral ribbon

Full-size templates on this page.

1 Make the flowers.   A-2 (see p. 33), R (see p. 40)

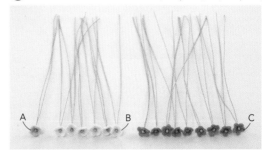

A   B   C

Thread 1 bead onto 1 length of wire and make the heart with 2 strands of wire. Punch 1 hole in the centre of the corolla, then insert the wire and glue in place. Make 1 A flower, 6 B flowers and 9 C flowers.

2 Make the leaves.   D (see p. 34)

Apply glue to the bottom of a leaf and glue 1 length of wire. Make 2 leaves.

3 Assemble the flower and the leaves.   S (see p. 40)

1

Assemble the B flowers, followed by the C flowers, around the A flower, forming a half-globe shape. Wrap with floral ribbon.

Full-size templates (#37)

Corolla x 26

Centre

Sewing guide

Leaf x 5

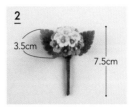

2

3.5cm

7.5cm

Join the flower and the leaves by wrapping floral ribbon around them. Cut excess wire and cover ends with floral ribbon.

Full-size templates (#39)

A corolla x 1
B corolla x 6
C corolla x 9

Centre

Leaf x 2

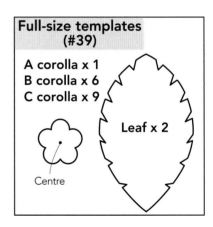

38. Moss Flox P. 13

a   b

Full-size templates below.

Supplies
Felt (from left to right: models a/b)
1 x 4 cm x 4 cm piece white/pink (corolla)
1 x 2 cm x 3 cm piece green/yellow-green (chalice)
4 x 2 cm x 3 cm pieces green/yellow-green (leaves)

Other supplies (for each model)
1 x 0.3 cm yellow bead (heart)
5 x 0.2 cm light yellow/red beads (corolla)
1 x 18 cm length of 0.37 mm steel wire (flower)
Green floral ribbon

① Make the heart.
A-1 (see p. 33)

Thread 1 bead onto 1 length of wire. Twist wire 2 or 3 times close to the bead.

② Make the flower.
F-3 (see p. 35)

1

Sew the beads onto the corolla and tighten.

R (see p. 40)

2

Punch 1 hole in the centre of the corolla. Insert the heart wire and glue in place.

③ Glue the chalice.

1

Apply glue to the chalice.

2

Glue to bottom of the flower.

④ Glue the leaves.
D (see p. 34)

1

1cm

Apply glue to the bottom of a leaf and glue to the flower.

2

Hold together with a clamp and leave to dry.

3

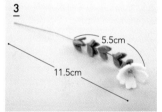

5.5cm

11.5cm

Glue the 3 remaining flowers in the same manner. Cut excess wire.

Full-size templates (#38)

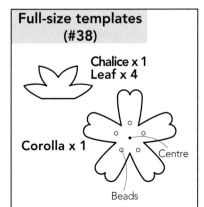

Chalice x 1
Leaf x 4

Corolla x 1

Centre

Beads

Full-size templates (#40)

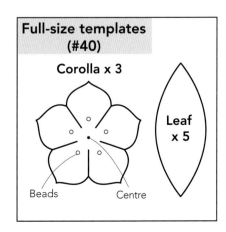

Corolla x 3

Leaf x 5

Beads   Centre

40. Madagascar Periwinkle P. 13

a

b

Supplies
Felt (from left to right: models a/b)
3 x 3.5 cm x 3.5 cm pieces light pink/red (corollas)
5 x 2.5 cm x 4.5 cm pieces dark green/very dark green (leaves)

Other supplies (for each model)
3 x 0.3 cm light yellow beads (hearts)
15 x 0.2 cm purple/white beads (corollas)
3 x 36 cm lengths of 0.37 mm steel wire (flowers)
5 x 18 cm lengths of 0.3 mm steel wire (leaves)
Green floral ribbon

Full-size templates on p. 75.

1 Make the flower.

N (see p. 38)

A-2 (see p. 33), F3 (see p. 35), R (see p. 40)

1

2

Apply glue to the ends of the petals and pinch.

Make 3 flowers as per model 2 on p. 44.

2 Make the leaves.

E (see p. 35)

Punch 1 hole through the thickness of the felt, then insert and glue 1 length of wire. Make 5 leaves.

3 Assemble the flower and the leaves.

S (see p. 40)

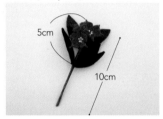

5cm

10cm

Join the flowers and the leaves by wrapping floral ribbon around them. Cut excess wire and cover ends with floral ribbon.

---

41. Ipheon Uniflorum P. 15

a

b

Supplies
Felt (from left to right: models a/b)
3 x 4 cm x 4 cm pieces light blue/light yellow (corollas)
5 x 2.5 cm x 4.5 cm pieces light green/yellow-green (leaves)

Other supplies (for each model)
3 x 0.3 cm olive beads (hearts)
15 x 0.2 cm yellow beads (corollas)
3 x 36 cm lengths of 0.37 mm steel wire (flowers)
5 x 18 cm lengths of 0.3 mm steel wire (flowers)
Green floral ribbon

Full-size templates on this page.

1 Make the flower.

A-2 (see p. 33)
F-3 (see p. 35), R (see p. 40)

Make 3 flowers as per model 2 on p. 44. Bring the 3 petals marked by a ★ forward.

2 Make the leaves.

E (see p. 35)

Punch 1 hole through the thickness of the felt, then insert and glue 1 length of wire. Make 5 leaves.

3 Assemble the flower and the leaves.

S (see p. 40)

6.5cm

11.5cm

Join the flowers and the leaves by wrapping floral ribbon around them. Cut excess wire and cover ends with floral ribbon.

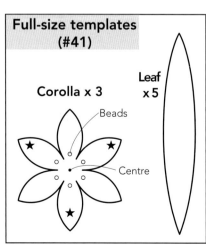
Full-size templates (#41)
Corolla x 3
Leaf x 5
Beads
Centre

42. Primrose P. 15

a

b

Full-size templates on this page.

Supplies
Felt (from left to right: models a/b)
6 x 2 cm x 2 cm pieces yellow (hearts)
6 x 3.5 cm x 3.5 cm pieces orange/blue (corollas)
5 x 4 cm x 5 cm pieces green/light green (leaves)

Other supplies (for each model)
6 x 0.3 cm olive beads (hearts)
6 x 36 cm lengths of 0.45 mm steel wire (flowers)
5 x 18 cm lengths of 0.3 mm steel wire (leaves)
Green floral ribbon

① Make the flowers.
F-2 (see p. 35)

A-2 (see p. 33), R (see p. 40)

1 Overlay the heart and the corolla and sew the centre.

2 Pull the thread to tighten.

3 Thread 1 bead onto 1 length of wire and make the heart with 2 stands of wire. Punch 1 hole in the flower from step 1-2 then insert the wire and glue in place. Make 6 flowers.

② Make the leaves.
E (see p. 35)

Punch 1 hole through the thickness of the felt, then insert and glue 1 length of wire. Make 5 leaves.

③ Assemble the flower and the leaves.
S (see p. 40)

7.5cm   10.5cm

Join the flowers and the leaves by wrapping floral ribbon around them. Cut excess wire and cover ends with floral ribbon.

Full-size templates (#42)

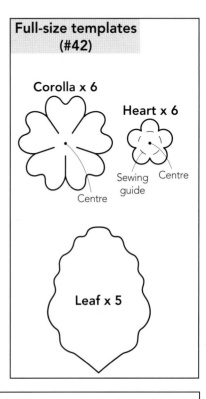

Corolla x 6

Heart x 6

Centre

Sewing guide   Centre

Centre

Leaf x 5

Full-size templates (#26)

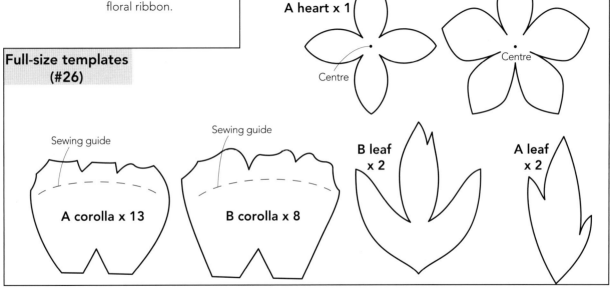

A heart x 1

Chalice x 2

Centre

Centre

Sewing guide

Sewing guide

A corolla x 13

B corolla x 8

B leaf x 2

A leaf x 2

77

43. Sweet Alyssum P. 15

a

b

Full-size templates on this page.

Supplies

Felt (from left to right: models a/b)

12 x 1.5 cm x 1.5 cm pieces pink/violet (corollas)

8 x 1.5 cm x 4 cm pieces green/yellow-green (leaves)

Other supplies (for each model)

6 x 0.3 cm yellow beads (A heart)

12 x 0.3 cm yellow beads (B hearts)

6 x 36 cm lengths of 0.3 mm steel wire (A heart)

12 x 36 cm lengths of 0.3 mm steel wire (B hearts)

8 x 18 cm lengths of 0.3 mm steel wire (leaves)

Green floral ribbon

1 Make the A heart.

A-2 (see p. 33)

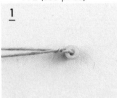

1

Thread 1 bead onto 1 length of wire, then twist the wire 2 or 3 times at the base of the bead. Make 6 components.

2

Assemble the 6 components from step 1-1 with floral ribbon (A heart).

2 Make the flowers.

A-2 (see p. 33), R (see p. 40)

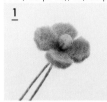

1

Thread 1 bead onto 1 length of wire, then make B heart with 2 strands of wire. Punch 1 hole in the centre of the corolla and insert B heart wire and glue in place. Make 12 flowers.

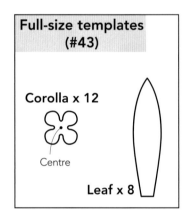

Full-size templates (#43)

Corolla x 12

Centre

Leaf x 8

2

Assemble the flowers around A heart with floral ribbon.

3 Make the leaves.

D (see p. 34)

Apply glue to the bottom of the leaf and glue 1 length of wire. Make 8 leaves. Join the leaves as follows: 2 components with 3 leaves and 1 component with 2 leaves.

4 Assemble the flowers and the leaves.

S (see p. 40)

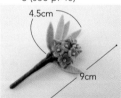

4.5cm

9cm

Join the flowers and the leaves by wrapping floral ribbon around them. Cut excess wire and cover ends with floral ribbon.

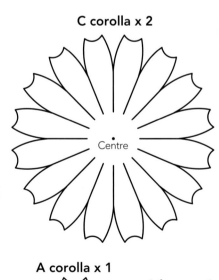

C corolla x 2

Centre

Full-size templates (#83)

B corolla x 4

A corolla x 1

Centre

A heart x 1
B heart x 1

Centre

Leaf x 7

Centre

44. Lobelia Erinus P. 15

a   b

Full-size templates below.

Supplies
Felt (from left to right: models a/b)
3 x 3.5 cm x 3.5 cm pieces red/purple (corollas)
5 x 2 cm x 4.5 cm pieces green/yellow-green (leaves)

Other supplies (for each model)
3 x 0.3 cm orange beads (hearts)
9 x 0.2 cm white beads (corollas)
3 x 18 cm lengths of 0.37 mm steel wire (flowers)
5 x 18 cm lengths of 0.3 mm steel wire (leaves)
Green floral ribbon

1 Make the flowers.

F-3 (see p. 35)   A-1 (see p. 33), R (see p. 40)

1   **2**   **3**   **4**

Sew 3 beads onto 3 petals and sew the 2 remaining petals without a bead.

Stitch into the 1st stitch.

Pull thread to tighten.

Thread 1 orange bead onto 1 length of wire and make the heart with 1 strand of wire. Punch 1 hole in the centre of the corolla, then insert the wire and glue in place. Make 3 flowers.

2 Make the leaves.

E (see p. 35)

Punch 1 hole through the thickness of the felt, then insert and glue 1 length of wire. Make 5 leaves.

3 Assemble the flower and the leaves.

S (see p. 40)

7cm
11.5cm

Join the flowers and the leaves by wrapping floral ribbon around them. Cut excess wire and cover ends with floral ribbon.

Full-size templates (#29)

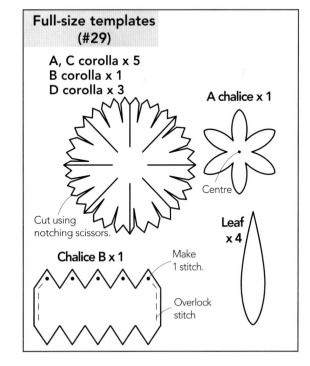

A, C corolla x 5
B corolla x 1
D corolla x 3

A chalice x 1

Centre

Cut using notching scissors.

Chalice B x 1

Make 1 stitch.

Overlock stitch

Leaf x 4

Full-size templates (#44)

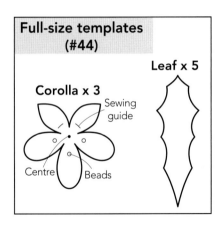

Corolla x 3

Leaf x 5

Sewing guide

Centre   Beads

45. White Clover, Red Clover P. 15

a

b

Full-size templates on this page.

Supplies
Felt (from left to right: models a/b)
3 x 3 cm x 3 cm pieces light green/dark red
(A corolla)
6 x 3 cm x 3 cm pieces white/magenta (B corolla)
1 x 3 cm x 3 cm piece yellow-green/dark green
(four-leaf clover)
2 x 3 cm x 3 cm pieces yellow-green/dark green (clover)

Other supplies (for each model)
5 x 0.3 cm yellow-green beads (four-leaf clover)
2 x 0.2 cm yellow-green beads (clovers)
6 x 0.3 cm yellow-green beads (clovers)
3 x 36 cm lengths of 0.3 mm steel wire (flowers)
3 x 36 cm lengths of 0.3 mm steel wire (leaves)
Green floral ribbon

1 Make the flowers.
J (see p. 37), R (see p. 40)

Fold A corolla twice, then attach 1 length of wire, folded in two. Twist wire 2 or 3 times at bottom of corolla. Punch 1 hole in the centre of the B corolla, then insert the wire and glue in place. Glue another B corolla. Make 3 flowers.

A-2 (see p. 33)

3

Thread 1 bead onto 1 length of wire and make the heart with 2 strands of wire. Punch 1 hole in the centre of the leaf, then insert the wire.

A-2 (see p. 33), R (see p. 40)

2
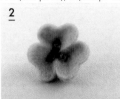

Pull thread to tighten. Thread 1 bead onto 1 length of wire and make the heart with 2 strands of wire. Punch 1 hole in the centre of the leaf, then insert the wire. Glue in place.

2 Make the four-leaf clover.
F-3 (see p. 35)

1
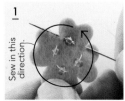
Sew in this direction.

Sew 1 bead onto each leaf, then stitch into the 1st stitch.

2

Pull thread to tighten.

3 Make the clovers.
F-3 (see p. 35)

1
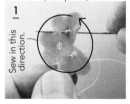
Sew in this direction.

Sew 1 bead onto each leaf.

4 Assemble the flower and the leaves.
S (see p. 40)

1

Join components as follows: 1 component with 2 flowers and 1 clover, 1 component with 1 flower and 1 clover, 1 four-leaf clover, wrapping them in floral ribbon.

2
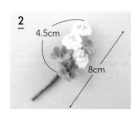
4.5cm
8cm

Assemble the components from step 4-1 by wrapping floral ribbon around them. Cut excess wire and cover ends with floral ribbon.

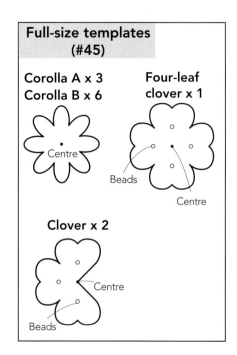
Full-size templates (#45)

Corolla A x 3
Corolla B x 6
Centre

Four-leaf clover x 1
Beads
Centre

Clover x 2
Centre
Beads

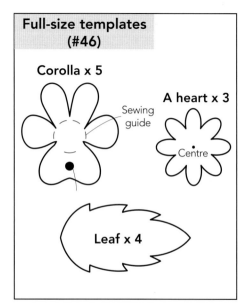
Full-size templates (#46)

Corolla x 5
Sewing guide

A heart x 3
Centre

Leaf x 4

46. Nemesia P. 15

a   b

Full-size templates on this page.

Supplies
Felt (from left to right: models a/b)
5 x 3.5 cm x 3.5 cm pieces pink/purple (corollas)
3 x 3 cm x 4.5 cm pieces yellow-green/green
(A hearts)
4 x 3 cm x 4.5 cm pieces yellow-green/green
(leaves)

Other supplies (for each model)
5 x 0.3 cm yellow/white beads (B hearts)
1 x 36 cm length of 0.3 mm steel wire (A heart)
5 x 36 cm lengths of 0.3 mm steel wire (B hearts)
4 x 18 cm lengths of 0.3 mm steel wire (leaves)
Green floral ribbon

---

1 Make the A heart.

J (see p. 37)   R (see p. 40)

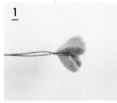

1
Fold A heart twice, then attach 1 length of wire, folded in two. Twist wire 2 or 3 times at bottom of A heart.

2
Punch 1 hole in the centre of the A heart, then insert the wire from step 1-1. Apply glue.

3
Glue in place.

4
Glue another A heart in the same manner.

2 Make the flowers.

F-1 (see p. 35)

1
Sew the centre of the corolla.

Sew in this direction.

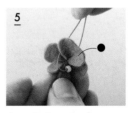

2
Stitch into 1st stitch.

3
Pull thread to tighten.

4
Thread 1 bead onto 1 length of wire and fold in 2 (B heart).

5
Attach the wire from step 2-4 to the ● part of the corolla.

6
Holding the petals, twist the wire 2 or 3 times at the bottom of the corolla.

---

3 Make the leaves.

E (see p. 35)

4 Assemble the flower and the leaves.

S (see p. 40)

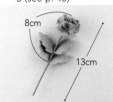

7
1 Flower is complete.

8
Make 5 flowers.

9
Join the flowers around the A heart, wrapping with floral ribbon.

Punch 1 hole through the thickness of the felt, then insert and glue 1 length of wire. Make 4 leaves.

8cm

13cm

Join the flower and the leaves by wrapping floral ribbon around them. Cut excess wire and cover ends with floral ribbon.

47. Sea Thrift P. 15

a   b

Supplies
Felt (from left to right: models a/b)
12 x 3 cm x 3 cm pieces dark orange/purple (corollas)

Other supplies (for each model)
10 x 36 cm length of 0.3 mm steel wire (flowers)
8 x 18 cm lengths of 0.3 mm steel wire (leaves)
Green floral ribbon

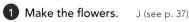

Full-size templates below.

1 Make the flowers.   J (see p. 37)

1

A   B

2

Fold corolla twice, then attach 1 length of wire, folded in two. Twist wire 2 or 3 times at bottom corolla (A).
Fold corolla once, then attach 1 length of wire, folded in two. Twist wire 2 or 3 times at bottom of corolla (B). Make 4 B components.

Assemble the B components around the A component.

3

4   R (see p. 40)

5

Twist the wires at the base of the corollas.

Punch 1 hole in the centre of the corolla and insert the wire from step 1-3. Apply glue to the bottom of the corolla.

Glue together then wrap in floral ribbon. Make 2 flowers.

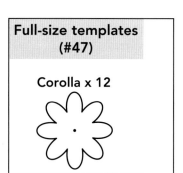

Full-size templates (#47)

Corolla x 12

2 Make the leaves.

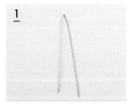

1

2

3 Assemble the flower and the leaves.
S (see p. 40)

1

approximately 7.5 cm.

Fold the length of wire in 2.

Wrap in floral ribbon. Make 8 components.

Assemble the 2 flowers and wrap in floral ribbon.

2

3

9.5cm
12.5cm

Join the flower and the leaves by wrapping floral ribbon around them.

Cut excess wire and cover ends with floral ribbon.

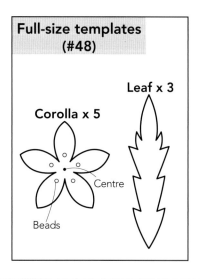

Full-size templates (#48)

Corolla x 5   Leaf x 3

Centre

Beads

48. Laurentia P. 15

a b

Full-size templates on p. 82

Supplies
Felt (from left to right: models a/b)
5 x 3.5 cm x 3.5 cm pieces light orange/blue (corollas)
3 x 2 cm x 5.5 cm pieces green/dark green (leaves)
Other supplies (for each model)
5 x 0.3 cm blue beads (hearts)
25 x 0.2 cm yellow beads (corollas)
5 x 36 cm lengths of 0.37 mm steel wire (flowers)
3 x 18 cm lengths of 0.3 mm steel wire (leaves)
Green floral ribbon

① Make the flower.
A-1 (see p. 33),
F-3 (see p. 35), R (see p. 40)

Thread 1 blue bead onto 1 length of wire and make the heart with 1 strand of wire. Sew 5 yellow beads to the bottom of the petals, then pull thread to tighten. Insert the heart wire in the centre of the corolla and glue together. Make 5 flowers.

② Make the leaves.
E (see p. 35)

Punch 1 hole through the thickness of the felt, then insert and glue 1 length of wire. Make 3 leaves.

③ Assemble the flower and the leaves.
S (see p. 40)

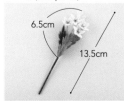

6.5cm
13.5cm

Join the flower and the leaves by wrapping floral ribbon around them. Cut excess wire and cover ends with floral ribbon.

Full-size templates (#12)

A heart exterior x 1
A heart interior x 1
B heart x 5

Centre

Corolla x 5

Leaf x 2

Full-size templates (#70)

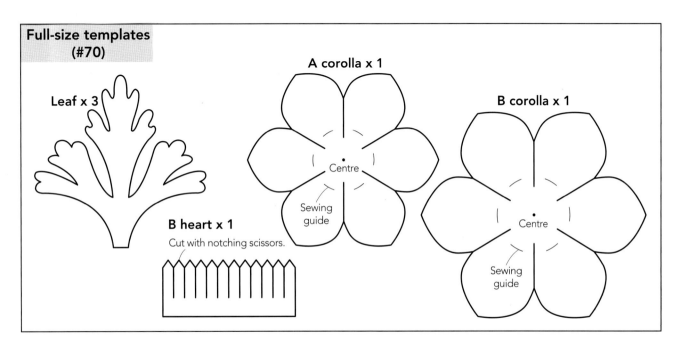

Leaf x 3

A corolla x 1

Centre

Sewing guide

B heart x 1
Cut with notching scissors.

B corolla x 1

Centre

Sewing guide

49. Siskiyou Lewisia P. 15

a  b

Full-size templates below.

Supplies
Felt (from left to right: models a/b)
6 x 3.5 cm x 3.5 cm pieces orange/light orange (corollas)
5 x 2.5 cm x 6 cm pieces green/yellow-green (leaves)

Other supplies (for each model)
3 x 0.3 cm orange/red beads (hearts)
3 x 36 cm lengths of 0.3 mm steel wire (flowers)
5 x 18 cm lengths of 0.3 mm steel wire (leaves)
Green floral ribbon

1 Make the flower.

A-2 (see p. 33),
F-2 (see p. 35), R (see p. 40)

Thread 1 bead onto 1 length of wire and make the heart with 2 strands of wire. Overlay 2 corollas and sew the centre. Pull the thread to tighten. Punch 1 hole in the centre of the corolla, then insert the heart wire and glue together. Make 3 flowers.

2 Make the leaves.

E (see p. 35)

Punch 1 hole through the thickness of the felt, then insert and glue 1 length of wire. Make 5 leaves.

3 Assemble the flower and the leaves.

S (see p. 40)

1

Assemble the 3 flowers and wrap in floral ribbon.

2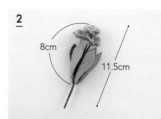

8cm
11.5cm

Join the flower and the leaves by wrapping floral ribbon around them. Cut excess wire and cover ends with floral ribbon.

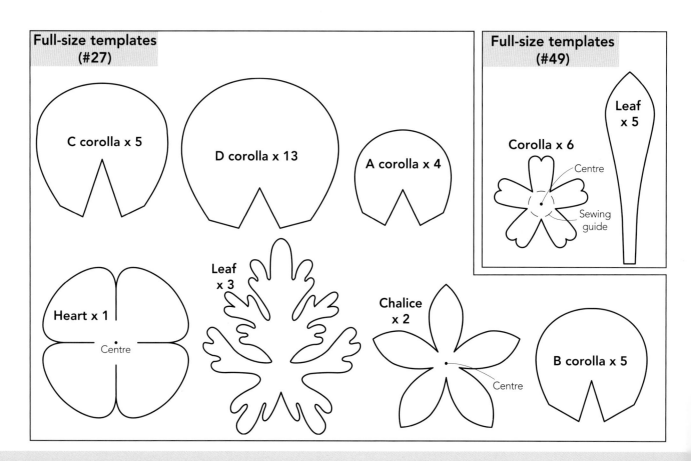

Full-size templates (#27)

C corolla x 5

D corolla x 13

A corolla x 4

Heart x 1
Centre

Leaf x 3

Chalice x 2
Centre

B corolla x 5

Full-size templates (#49)

Leaf x 5

Corolla x 6
Centre
Sewing guide

50. Sweet William Catchfly P. 15

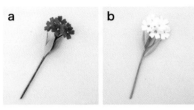
a   b

Supplies
Felt (from left to right: models a/b)
6 x 4 cm x 4 cm pieces pink/light yellow
(corollas)
3 x 2 cm x 4 cm pieces green/yellow-green
(leaves)

Other supplies (for each model)
6 x 0.3 cm pink/yellow beads (hearts)
6 x 36 cm lengths of 0.3 mm steel wire (flowers)
3 x 18 cm lengths of 0.3 mm steel wire (leaves)
Green floral ribbon

Full-size templates below.

1 Make the hearts.
A-2 (see p. 33)

Thread 1 bead onto 1 length
of wire and twist 2 or 3 times
at the bottom of the bead.

2 Make the flowers.
F-1 (see p. 35), R (see p. 40)

1

Sew the centre of the corolla
and tighten. Punch 1 hole in
the centre and insert the wire.

2

Apply glue and glue
together. Make 6 flowers.

3 Make the leaves.
E (see p. 35)

Punch 1 hole through the
thickness of the felt, then
insert and glue 1 length of
wire. Make 3 leaves.

4 Assemble the flower and the leaves.
S (see p. 40)

1

Wrap floral ribbon around
each stem.

2

5.5cm
12.5cm

Join the flower and the leaves
by wrapping floral ribbon
around them. Cut excess wire
and cover ends with
floral ribbon.

**Full-size templates
(#50)**

Leaf x 3

Corolla x 6

Centre

Sewing
guide

**Full-size templates
(#62)**

a, b (for each color)
A corolla x 3

Sewing
guide

Punch
1 hole

a, b (for each color)
B corolla x 3

Punch 1 hole

a: leaf x 2
b: leaf x 9

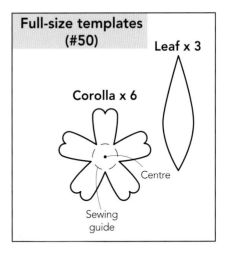

51. Oxalis P. 15

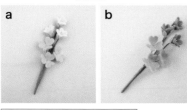

a   b

Full-size templates below.

Supplies
Felt (from left to right: models a/b)

3 x 3.5 cm x 3.5 cm pieces yellow/pink (corollas)

3 x 3 cm x 3 cm pieces yellow-green/light green (chalices)

9 x 2 cm x 2 cm pieces yellow-green/light green (leaves)

Other supplies (for each model)
3 x 0.3 cm yellow-green beads (hearts)

3 x 36 cm lengths of 0.3 mm steel wire (flowers)

9 x 18 cm lengths of 0.3 mm steel wire (leaves)

Green floral ribbon

❶ Make the flowers.
F-1 (see p. 35)   A-2 (see p. 33), R (see p. 40)

1

Sew then centre of the corolla. Pull thread to tighten.

2

Thread 1 bead onto 1 length of wire and make the heart with 2 strands of wire. Punch 1 hole in the centre of the corolla, then insert the heart wire and glue together.

❷ Glue the chalices.
R (see p. 40)

Punch 1 hole in the centre of the chalice, then insert the corolla wire and glue together. Make 3 flowers.

❸ Make the leaves.
E (see p. 35)

1

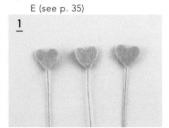

Punch 1 hole through the thickness of the felt, then insert and glue 1 length of wire. Make 9 leaves.

❹ Assemble the flower and the leaves.
S (see p. 40)

2

Bend the wire at a 90-degree angle below the leaf. Assemble 3 leaves and glue together. Make 3 identical components.

1

Wrap floral ribbon around each stem.

2

6.5cm

10.5cm

Join the flowers and the leaves by wrapping floral ribbon around them. Cut excess wire and cover ends with floral ribbon.

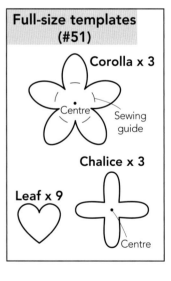

Full-size templates (#51)

Corolla x 3

Centre   Sewing guide

Chalice x 3

Leaf x 9

Centre

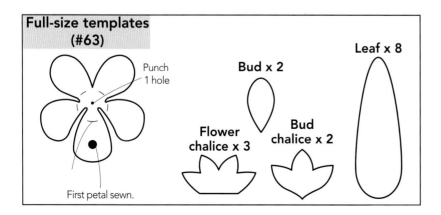

Full-size templates (#63)

Punch 1 hole

First petal sewn.

Bud x 2

Leaf x 8

Flower chalice x 3

Bud chalice x 2

52. Geranium P. 15

a b

Full-size templates on this page.

Supplies
Felt (from left to right: models a/b)
2 x 3.5 cm x 3.5 cm pieces violet/pink (corollas)
3 x 4 cm x 5 cm pieces green/yellow-green (leaves)

Other supplies (for each model)
2 x 0.3 cm yellow beads (hearts)
10 x 0.3 cm pink/light pink beads (corollas)
2 x 36 cm lengths of 0.37 mm steel wire (flowers)
3 x 18 cm lengths of 0.3 mm steel wire (leaves)
Green floral ribbon

1 Make the flowers.

A-2 (see p. 33),
F-3 (see p. 35), R (see p. 40)

Make the heart with 2 strands of wire. Sew 5 beads to the centre of the corolla, then punch 1 hole. Insert the heart wire. Make 2 flowers.

2 Make the leaves.

E (see p. 35)

Punch 1 hole through the thickness of the felt, then insert and glue 1 length of wire. Make 3 leaves.

3 Assemble the flower and the leaves.

S (see p. 40)

6cm
12cm

Join the flowers and the leaves by wrapping floral ribbon around them. Cut excess wire and cover ends with floral ribbon.

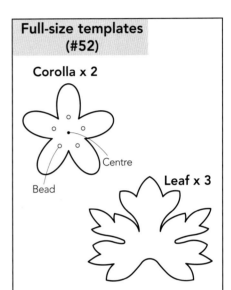

Full-size templates (#52)

Corolla x 2

Centre
Bead

Leaf x 3

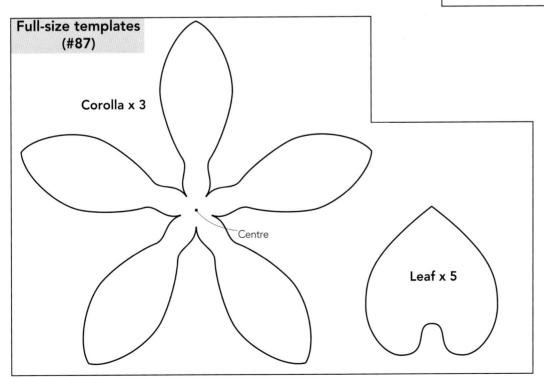

Full-size templates (#87)

Corolla x 3

Centre

Leaf x 5

53. Sutera P. 15

a

b

Supplies

Felt (from left to right: models a/b)

3 x 3.5 cm x 3.5 cm pieces pink/purple
(corollas)

9 x 2 cm x 2.5 cm pieces green/yellow-green
(leaves)

Other supplies (for each model)

3 x 0.3 cm yellow beads (hearts)

3 x 36 cm lengths of 0.3 mm steel wire (flowers)

9 x 18 cm lengths of 0.3 mm steel wire (leaves)

Green floral ribbon

Full-size templates on this page.

① Make the flowers.

A-2 (see p. 33),
F-1 (see p. 35), R (see p. 40)

Thread 1 bead onto 1 length of wire and make the heart with 2 strands of wire. Sew the centre of the corolla, then pull the thread to tighten. Punch 1 hole in the centre of the corolla and insert the heart wire and glue in place. Make 3 flowers.

② Make the leaves.

E (see p. 35)

Punch 1 hole through the thickness of the felt, then insert and glue 1 length of wire. Make 9 leaves.

③ Assemble the flower and the leaves.

S (see p. 40)

1

Assemble 1 flower and 3 leaves by wrapping floral ribbon around them. Make 3 identical components.

2

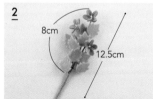
8cm 12.5cm

Join the components from step 3-1 by wrapping floral ribbon around them. Cut excess wire and cover ends with floral ribbon.

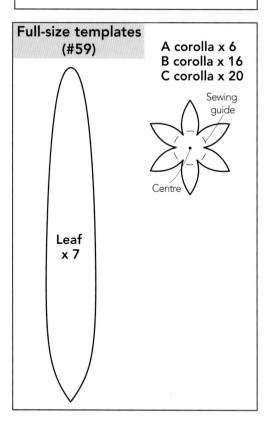

Full-size templates (#53)

Corolla x 3

Centre

Sewing guide

Leaf x 9

Full-size templates (#59)

A corolla x 6
B corolla x 16
C corolla x 20

Sewing guide

Centre

Leaf x 7

Full-size templates (#60)

Corolla x 30

Sewing guide

Centre

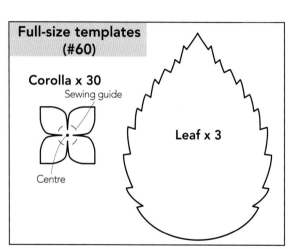

Leaf x 3

54. Astrantia P. 15

Full-size templates on this page.

Supplies
Felt (from left to right: models a/b)
6 x 3 cm x 3 cm pieces dark pink/light yellow (flower hearts)
6 x 4 cm x 4 cm pieces light pink/light blue (corollas)
2 x 3 cm x 3 cm pieces dark pink/light yellow (bud hearts)
2 x 3.5 cm x 3.5 cm pieces light pink/light blue (chalices)
2 x 4 cm x 5.5 cm pieces yellow-green/green (leaves)

Other supplies (for each model)
3 x 36 cm lengths of 0.3 mm steel wire (flowers)
2 x 36 cm lengths of 0.3 mm steel wire (buds)
2 x 18 cm lengths of 0.3 mm steel wire (leaves)
Green floral ribbon

1 Make the hearts.
J (see p. 37)

1

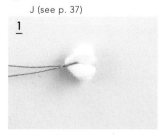

Fold the flower heart twice and attach 1 length of wire, folded in two. Twist the wire 2 or 3 times at the bottom of the heart.

R (see p. 40)

2

Punch 1 hole in the centre of another flower heart, then insert the wire from step 1-1 and glue in place.

2 Make the flower.

1

Punch 1 hole in the centre of the corolla, then insert the heart wire and glue in place.

2

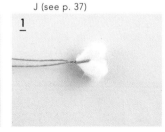

Glue another corolla, staggering the petals. Make 3 flowers.

3 Make the buds.
J (see p. 37)

1

Fold the bud heart twice and attach 1 length of wire, folded in two. Twist the wire 2 or 3 times at the bottom of the heart.

R (see p. 40)

2

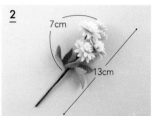

Punch 1 hole in the centre of the chalice, then insert the wire from step 3-1 and glue in place. Make 2 buds.

4 Make the leaves.
D (see p. 34)

Apply glue to the bottom of the leaf, then glue 1 length of wire. Make 2 leaves.

5 Assemble the flowers and the leaves.
S (see p. 40)

1

Assemble the flowers and the buds by wrapping them in floral ribbon.

2

7cm

13cm

Join the component from step 5-1 and the leaves by wrapping floral ribbon around them. Cut excess wire and cover ends with floral ribbon.

Full-size templates (#54)

Flower heart x 6
Bud heart x 2

Centre

Bud chalice x 2

Centre

Flower corolla x 6

Centre

Leaf x 2

55. Lilac P. 16

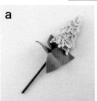
a

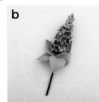
b

Full-size templates below.

Supplies
Felt (from left to right: models a/b)
30 x 3 cm x 3 cm pieces light pink/purple (corollas)
9 x 3 cm x 3 cm pieces light pink/purple (buds)
5 x 5 cm x 5 cm pieces green/yellow-green (leaves)

Other supplies (for each model)
30 x 0.2 cm yellow beads (hearts)
9 x 0.4 cm beige wooden beads (buds)
30 x 18 cm lengths of 0.3 mm steel wire (flowers)
9 x 18 cm lengths of 0.3 mm steel wire (buds)
5 x 18 cm lengths of 0.45 mm steel wire (leaves)
Green floral ribbon

① Make the flowers.

A-1 (see p. 33),
F-1 (see p. 35), R (see p. 40)

Thread 1 yellow bead onto 1 length of wire and make the heart with 1 strand of wire. Sew the centre of the corolla and pull the thread to tighten. Punch 1 hole in the centre of the corolla, insert the wire and glue in place. Make 30 flowers.

② Make the buds.

A-1 (see p. 33)

1
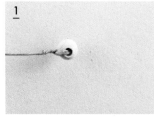

Thread 1 wooden bead onto 1 length of wire, then twist the wire 2 or 3 times at the bottom of the bead. Cut excess wire.

C-1 (see p. 34)

2

Punch 1 hole in the centre of the bud, then insert the heart wire. Apply glue to the bottom of the bead.

3

Glue together. Make 9 buds.

③ Make the leaves.

E (see p. 35)

Punch 1 hole through the thickness of the felt, then insert and glue 1 length of wire. Make 5 leaves.

④ Assemble the flowers, buds, and leaves.

S (see p. 40)

1

Assemble the buds in a triangle shape.

2

Wrap in floral ribbon.

3

8cm

Join the flowers around the buds and wrap floral ribbon around them.

4
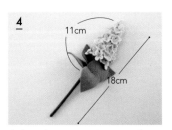

11cm

18cm

Join the component from step 4-3 and the leaves by wrapping floral ribbon around them. Cut excess wire and cover ends with floral ribbon.

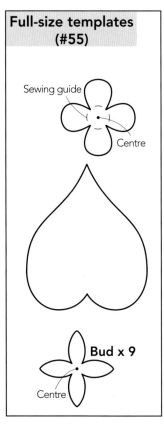

Full-size templates (#55)

Sewing guide

Centre

18cm

Bud x 9

Centre

56. Viburnum P. 16

Supplies
Felt
30 x 3 cm x 3 cm pieces light green (corollas)
3 x 5 cm x 5 cm pieces green (leaves)

Other supplies
30 x 0.3 cm light green beads (hearts)
30 x 18 cm lengths of 0.3 mm steel wire (flowers)
3 x 18 cm lengths of 0.37 mm steel wire (leaves)
Green floral ribbon

Full-size templates below.

1 Make the flowers.

A-1 (see p. 33),
F-1 (see p. 35), R (see p. 40)

Thread 1 bead onto 1 length of wire and make the heart with 1 strand of wire. Sew the centre of the corolla and pull the thread to tighten. Punch 1 hole in the centre of the corolla, insert the heart wire and glue in place. Make 30 flowers.

2 Make the leaves.

E (see p. 35)

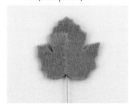

Punch 1 hole through the thickness of the felt, then insert and glue 1 length of wire. Make 3 leaves.

3 Assemble the flowers and the leaves.

S (see p. 40)

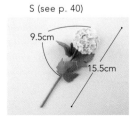

Join the leaves to form a globe and wrap in floral ribbon. Join the leaves, cut excess wire and cover ends with floral ribbon.

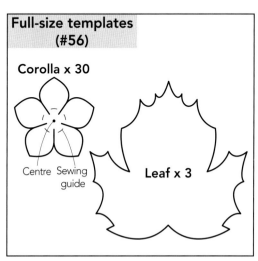

Full-size templates (#56)

Corolla x 30

Centre Sewing guide

Leaf x 3

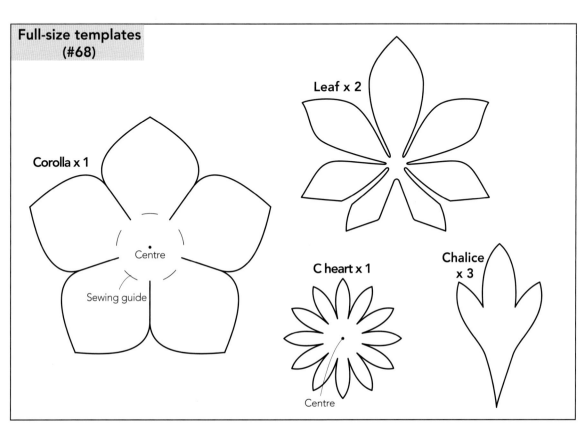

Full-size templates (#68)

Corolla x 1

Centre

Sewing guide

Leaf x 2

C heart x 1

Centre

Chalice x 3

57. Phlox P. 16

a

b

Supplies (from left to right: models a/b)
Felt
8 x 3.5 cm x 3.5 cm pieces off-white/light pink (corollas)
4 x 2.5 cm x 7 cm pieces yellow-green/green (leaves)

Other supplies (for each model)
8 x 0.3 cm yellow beads (hearts)
8 x 36 cm lengths of 0.3 mm steel wire (flowers)
4 x 18 cm lengths of 0.3 mm steel wire (leaves)
Green floral ribbon

Full-size templates on this page.

1 Make the flower.
A-2 (see p. 33),
F-1 (see p. 35), R (see p. 40)

Thread 1 bead onto 1 length of wire and make the heart with 2 strands of wire. Sew the centre of the corolla and pull the thread to tighten. Punch 1 hole in the centre of the corolla, insert the heart wire and glue in place. Make 8 flowers.

2 Make the leaves.
E (see p. 35)

Punch 1 hole through the thickness of the felt, then insert and glue 1 length of wire. Make 4 leaves.

3 Assemble the flowers and the leaves.
S (see p. 40)

6.5cm
13cm

Join the flowers and the leaves and wrap them in floral ribbon. Cut excess wire and cover ends with floral ribbon.

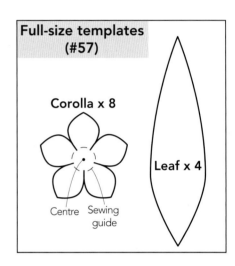

Full-size templates (#57)

Corolla x 8

Leaf x 4

Centre   Sewing guide

60. Hydrangea P. 17

a

b

Supplies (from left to right: models a/b)
Felt
30 x 2.5 cm x 2.5 cm pieces coral/light blue (corollas)
3 x 5 cm x 6.5 cm pieces yellow-green/dark green (leaves)

Other supplies (for each model)
30 x 0.2 cm dark pink/turquoise beads (hearts)
30 x 18 cm lengths of 0.3 mm steel wire (flowers)
3 x 18 cm lengths of 0.45 mm steel wire (leaves)
Green floral ribbon

Full-size templates on p. 88.

1 Make the flowers.
A-1 (see p. 33),
F-1 (see p. 35), R (see p. 40)

Make the heart with 1 strand of wire. Sew the centre of the corolla and pull the thread to tighten. Punch 1 hole in the centre, insert the heart wire and glue in place. Make 30 flowers.

2 Make the leaves.
E (see p. 35)

Punch 1 hole through the thickness of the felt, then insert and glue 1 length of wire. Make 3 leaves.

3 Assemble the flowers and the leaves.
S (see p. 40)

1

Assemble the flowers in a half-globe shape and wrap in floral ribbon.

2
6cm
11cm

Join the flowers and the leaves and wrap them in floral ribbon. Cut excess wire and cover ends with floral ribbon.

58. Plumbago Auriculata P. 17

Full-size templates below.

Supplies

Felt

13 x 3 cm x 3 cm pieces light blue (corollas)

5 x 2.5 cm x 3.5 cm pieces light green (leaves)

Other supplies

13 x 0.3 cm white beads (hearts)

13 x 18 cm lengths of 0.3 mm steel wire (flowers)

5 x 18 cm lengths of 0.3 mm steel wire (leaves)

Green floral ribbon

1 Make the flowers.

A-2 (see p. 33),

F-1 (see p. 35), R (see p. 40)

1 Thread 1 bead onto 1 length of wire and make the heart with 2 strands of wire. Sew the centre of the corolla and pull thread to tighten. Punch 1 hole in the centre of the corolla, insert the heart wire and glue in place. Make 13 flowers.

2 Assemble 5 flowers around 1 flower and wrap in floral ribbon.

3 Assemble 7 flowers around the 1-2 component, forming a half globe, and wrap in floral ribbon.

2 Make the leaves.

E (see p. 35)

1 Punch 1 hole through the thickness of the felt, then insert and glue 1 length of wire. Make 5 leaves.

2 Assemble 2 leaves and wrap in floral ribbon. Make 2 components with 2 leaves and 1 component with 1 leaf.

3 Assemble the flowers and the leaves.

S (see p. 40)

6.5cm

12.5cm

Join the flowers and the leaves and wrap them in floral ribbon. Cut excess wire and cover ends with floral ribbon.

Full-size templates (#58)

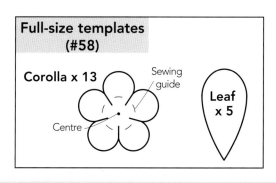

Corolla x 13

Sewing guide

Centre

Leaf x 5

Full-size template (#65)

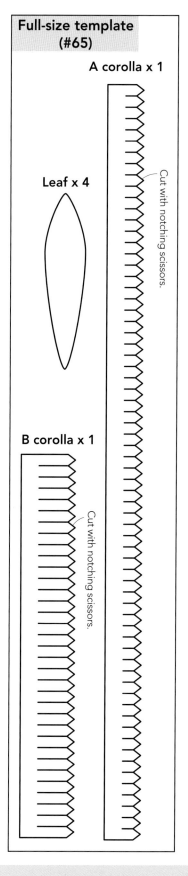

A corolla x 1

Leaf x 4

B corolla x 1

Cut with notching scissors.

Cut with notching scissors.

59. Hyacinth P. 17

a   b

Full-size templates on p. 88.

Supplies (from left to right: models a/b)
Felt

6 x 3 cm x 3 cm pieces dark blue/light orange (A corollas)

16 x 3 cm x 3 cm pieces blue/light yellow (B corollas)

20 x 3 cm x 3 cm pieces light blue/light yellow (C corollas)

7 x 2.5 cm x 10 cm pieces dark green/green (leaves)

Other supplies

42 x 0.2 cm blue/yellow beads (hearts)

42 x 18 cm lengths of 0.3 mm steel wire (flowers)

7 x 18 cm lengths of 0.45 mm steel wire (leaves)

Green floral ribbon

① Make the flowers.

A-1 (see p. 33)
F-1 (see p. 35), R (see p. 40)

1

Thread 1 bead onto 1 length of wire and make the heart with 1 strand of wire. Sew the centre of the corolla and pull thread to tighten. Punch 1 hole in the centre of the corolla, insert the heart wire and glue in place. Make 6 A flowers, 16 B flowers and 20 C flowers.

2

Assemble A flowers into a half globe and wrap in floral ribbon.

3

Assemble B flowers under the A flowers and wrap in floral ribbon.

6cm

Assemble C flowers under the B flowers and wrap in floral ribbon.

② Make the leaves.

N (see p. 38)

1

Apply glue to the top of the leaf.

2

Pinch the top of the leaf and hold in place with a clamp. Leave to dry.

E (see p. 35)

3

Punch 1 hole through the thickness of the felt, then insert and glue 1 length of wire. Make 7 leaves.

③ Assemble the flowers and the leaves.

S (see p. 40)

11cm

16cm

Join the flowers and the leaves and wrap them in floral ribbon. Cut excess wire and cover ends with floral ribbon.

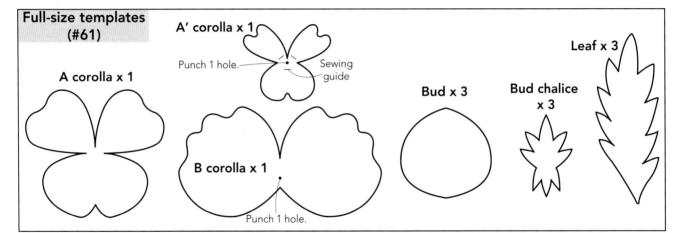

Full-size templates (#61)

A' corolla x 1
Punch 1 hole.   Sewing guide

A corolla x 1

B corolla x 1
Punch 1 hole.

Bud x 3

Bud chalice x 3

Leaf x 3

61. Pansy P. 18

a

b

c

Full-size templates on p. 94.

Supplies (from left to right: models a/b/c)
Felt
1 x 5 cm x 5 cm piece purple/light blue/yellow (A corolla)
1 x 3.5 cm x 3.5 cm piece dark purple/dark blue/maroon (A' corolla)
1 x 4 cm x 6.5 cm piece purple/blue/pink (B corolla)
3 x 3 cm x 3 cm pieces purple/blue/pink (buds)
3 x 2 cm x 3 cm pieces green (chalices)
3 x 2.5 cm x 5.5 cm pieces green (leaves)
Other supplies (for each model)
1 x 0.3 cm yellow bead (heart)
1 x 36 cm length of 0.37 mm steel wire (flower)
3 x 18 cm lengths of 0.45 mm steel wire (buds)
3 x 18 cm lengths of 0.45 mm steel wire (leaves)
Green floral ribbon

1 Make the flower.

F-2 (see p. 35)

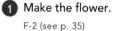

1

Overlay the A' corolla over the A corolla, then sew the centres of the corollas (see steps 1-1 and 2 of model 62 on p. 96).

2

Make the flower as per steps 1-3 to 9 of model 62 on p. 96.

3

approximately 1 cm

Wrap floral ribbon around bottom of flower, then curve the stem.

2 Make the buds.

1

0.5cm

Apply glue to the bottom of the bud and glue 1 length of wire.

2

Pinch the sides of the bud and hold in place with a clamp.

3

Apply glue to the bottom of the bud.

4

Pinch more and hold in place with a clamp.

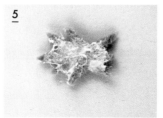

5

Apply glue to the chalice.

6

Glue the bud to the chalice.

7

Roll the chalice around the bud and hold in place with a clamp.

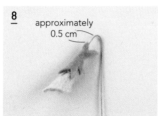

8

approximately 0.5 cm

Bend the stem. Make 3 buds.

3 Make the leaves.

E (see p. 35)

Punch 1 hole through the thickness of the felt, then insert and glue 1 length of wire. Make 3 leaves.

4 Assemble the flowers, buds, and leaves.

S (see p. 40)

9cm

13.5cm

Join the flower, buds, and leaves and wrap them in floral ribbon. Cut excess wire and cover ends with floral ribbon.

62. Violet P. 18

a

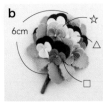
b
6cm

Full-size templates on p. 85.

Supplies
Felt and beads (model A)
3 x 3.5 cm x 3.5 cm pieces purple (A corollas)
3 x 3 cm x 4.5 cm pieces light blue (B corollas)
2 x 3.5 cm x 4 cm pieces yellow-green (leaves)
3 x 0.3 cm yellow beads (hearts)
Felt and beads (model B, ☆)
3 x 3.5 cm x 3.5 cm pieces purple (A corollas)
3x 3 cm x 4.5 cm pieces light blue (B corollas)
3 x 0.3 cm yellow beads (hearts)
Felt and beads (model B, △)
3 x 3.5 cm x 3.5 cm pieces yellow (A corollas)

3 x 3 cm x 4.5 cm pieces violet (B corollas)
3 x 0.3 cm orange beads (hearts)
Felt and beads (model B, □)
3 x 3.5 cm x 3.5 cm pieces orange (A corollas)
3 x 3 cm x 4.5 cm dark red (B corollas)
3 x 0.3 cm yellow beads (hearts)
Felt (model B)
9 x 3.5 cm x 4 cm pieces yellow-green (leaves)
Other supplies (for each model a/b)
3/9 x 36 cm length of 0.3 mm steel wire (flowers
2/9 x 18 cm lengths of 0.3 mm steel wire (leaves
Green floral ribbon

1 Make the flower.
F-1 (see p. 35)   A-2 (see p. 33), R (see p. 40)

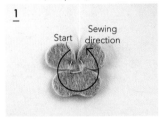
1
Start   Sewing direction

2

3

4

Sew the centre of the A corolla, without sewing into the 1st stitch after the last one.

Pull the thread to tighten.

Thread 1 bead onto 1 length of wire and make the heart with 2 strands of wire. Punch 1 hole in the corolla, then insert the heart wire.

Apply glue to the bottom of the bead and glue together.

5

6

7

8

Apply glue to the B corolla.

Overlay the edges of the petals and pin in place. Leave to dry.

Punch 1 hole as per the guide.

Insert the wire from step 1-4. Apply glue to the bottom of the B corolla.

2 Make the leaves.
E (see p. 35)

3 Assemble the flowers and the leaves.
S (see p. 40)

9

10

4.5cm
11cm

Glue together.

Wrap in floral ribbon, then curve the stem at a 90-degree angle. Make 3 flowers (model a)/3 flowers for each color ☆, △, □ for model b).

Punch 1 hole through the thickness of the felt, then insert and glue 1 length of wire. Make 2 leaves (model a)/9 leaves (model b).

Join the flower and the leaves and wrap them in floral ribbon. Cut excess wire and cover ends with floral ribbon.

63. Viola Mandshurica P. 18

Supplies

Felt

3 x 4 cm x 4 cm pieces dark purple (corollas)

3 x 2 cm x 3 cm pieces dark green (flower chalices)

2 x 1.5 cm x 2.5 cm pieces dark purple (buds)

2 x 2.5 cm x 2.5 cm pieces dark green (bud chalices)

8 x 2.5 cm x 5 cm pieces dark green (leaves)

Other supplies

3 x white 0.3 cm beads (hearts)

3 x 36 cm length of 0.3 mm steel wire (flowers)

2 x 18 cm lengths of 0.3 mm steel wire (buds)

8 x 18 cm lengths of 0.3 mm steel wire (leaves)

Green floral ribbon

Full-size templates on p. 86.

1 Make the flower.

F-1 (see p. 35)

1

Sew and tighten the centre of the corolla, as per model 46 on p. 81.

A-2 (see p. 33), R (see p. 40)

2

Thread 1 bead onto 1 length of wire and make the heart with 2 strands of wire. Punch 1 hole in the corolla as per the template, then insert the heart wire and glue together.

2 Glue the chalice.

1

Apply glue to the flower chalice.

2

Glue the chalice to the back of the flower. Make 3 flowers.

3 Make the buds.

D (see p. 34)

1

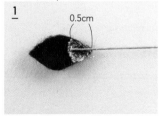

0.5cm

Apply glue to the bottom of the bud and glue 1 length of wire.

2

Pinch the bottom of the bud and hold with a clamp. Leave to dry.

3

Apply glue to the bud chalice and glue to the bottom of the bud. Make 2 buds.

4 Make the leaves.

E (see p. 35)

Punch 1 hole through the thickness of the felt, then insert and glue 1 length of wire. Make 8 leaves.

5 Assemble the flowers and the leaves.

S (see p. 40)

1

Wrap each stem in floral ribbon.

2

Fold the bottom of the flowers and of the buds at a 90-degree angle.

3

Join the flowers and the buds and wrap them in floral ribbon.

4

9cm

13cm

Join the component from step 5-3 and the leaves and wrap them in floral ribbon. Cut excess wire and cover ends with floral ribbon.

64. Acalypha Hispida, the Chenille Plant P. 20

Supplies
Felt
2 x 1 cm x 19.8 cm pieces dark red (A corollas)
2 x 1.5 cm x 19.8 cm pieces dark red (B corollas)
6 x 2.5 cm x 3.5 cm pieces green (leaves)
Other supplies
2 x 36 cm lengths of 0.55 mm steel wire (flowers)
6 x 18 cm lengths of 0.55 mm steel wire (leaves)
Green floral ribbon

Full-size templates below.

1 Make the flower.

G-1 (see p. 36)

1

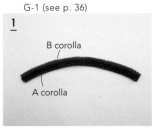

B corolla

A corolla

Cut 1 long side of the A and B corollas with the notching scissors, then notch. Overlay the corollas, then sew along the unnotched long side.

L (see p. 38)

2

Attach 1 length of wire, folded in 2, to the end of the corollas. Twist the wire at the bottom of the corollas.

3

5cm

Apply glue and roll the corollas in a spiral, with the B corolla on the outside. Make 2 flowers.

2 Make the leaves.

E (see p. 35)

Punch 1 hole through the thickness of the felt, then insert and glue 1 length of wire. Make 6 leaves.

3 Assemble the flowers and the leaves.

S (see p. 40)

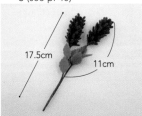

17.5cm

11cm

Join 1 flower and 3 leaves and wrap in floral ribbon. Make 2 identical components and join them by wrapping them in floral ribbon. Cut excess wire and cover ends with floral ribbon.

Full-size template (#64)

A corolla x 2	B corolla x 2
Cut with notching scissors.	Cut with notching scissors.

Leaf x 6

65. Veronica P. 20

Supplies
Felt
1 x 1 cm x 19.8 cm piece yellow-green (A corolla)
1 x 1.5 cm x 10.2 cm piece pink (B corolla)
1 x 3 cm x 20 cm piece pink (C corolla)
4 x 2 cm x 6 cm pieces yellow-green (leaves)

Other supplies
1 x 36 cm length of 0.55 mm steel wire (flower)
4 x 18 cm lengths of 0.55 mm steel wire (leaves)
Green floral ribbon

Full-size templates p. 93

1 Make the flower.

G-1 (see p. 36)

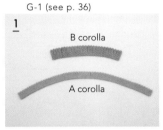

1
B corolla
A corolla

Cut 1 long side of the A and B corollas with the notching scissors, then notch.

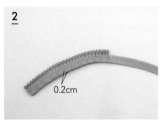

2
0.2cm

Overlay the corollas, then sew along the unnotched long side.

L (see p. 38)

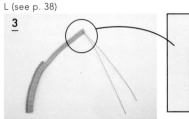

3

Attach 1 length of wire, folded in 2, to the end of the corollas. Twist the wire 2 or 3 times at the bottom of the corollas.

4

Apply glue to the A corolla and roll in a spiral, with the B corolla on the outside.

5

Continue to apply glue and roll in a spiral.

6
4cm

Pin the end of the corollas and leave to dry.

G-2 (see p. 36)

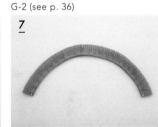

7

Fold the C corolla in 2, then sew long side. Notch over 1.1 cm, 0.3 cm apart.

L (see p. 38)

8

Apply glue and roll the C corolla in a spiral starting at the bottom of the 1-6 component.

9
8.5cm

Pin the end of the C corolla and leave to dry.

2 Make the leaves.

E (see p. 35)

Punch 1 hole through the thickness of the felt, then insert and glue 1 length of wire. Make 4 leaves.

3 Assemble the flower and the leaves.

S (see p. 40)

13.5cm
20.5cm

Join the flower and the leaves by wrapping them in floral ribbon. Cut excess wire and cover ends with floral ribbon.

66. Lavender P. 20

Supplies

Felt

1 x 4 cm x 4 cm piece violet (A corolla)

1 x 2 cm x 20 cm piece dark violet (B corolla)

4 x 2 cm x 3.5 cm pieces green (leaves)

Other supplies

1 x 36 cm length of 0.55 mm steel wire (flower)

Green floral ribbon

Full-size templates below.

1 Make the flower.

J (see p. 37)

1

Fold the A corolla twice, then attach 1 length of wire, folded in 2. Twist the wire 2 or 3 times and the bottom of the corolla.

G-2 (see p. 36)

2

Fold the B corolla in 2, then sew 1 long side. Notch on the bias over 0.8 cm, 0.3 cm apart.

L (see p. 38)

3

Apply glue and glue the A corolla to the edge of the B corolla.

4

Roll the B corolla in a spiral.

5

6cm

Pin the end of the B corolla and leave to dry.

2 Glue the leaves.

D (see p. 34)

1

0.5cm

Apply glue to the bottom of the leaf.

2

Glue the leaf to the bottom of the flower.

3

Hold in place with a clamp and leave to dry.

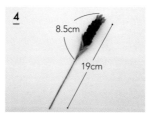

4

8.5cm

19cm

Glue the 3 remaining leaves in the same manner and wrap in floral ribbon. Cut excess wire and cover ends with floral ribbon.

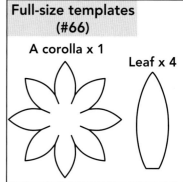

Full-size templates (#66)

A corolla x 1

Leaf x 4

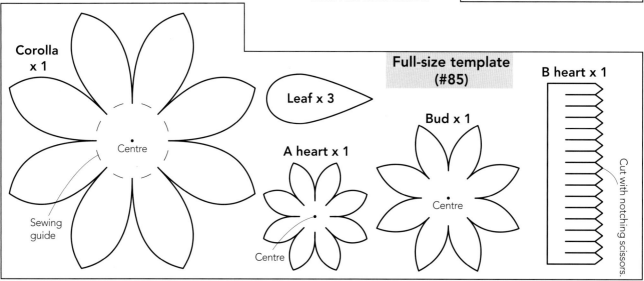

Corolla x 1

Centre

Sewing guide

Leaf x 3

A heart x 1

Centre

Full-size template (#85)

Bud x 1

Centre

B heart x 1

Cut with notching scissors.

67. Grape Hyacinth P. 20

 **a** **b** 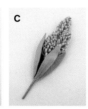 **c**  **d**

Supplies

Felt (from left to right, models a/c)
3 x 4 cm x 20 cm pieces sky blue/light blue (flowers)
5 x 2.5 cm x 10 cm pieces green/light green (leaves)
Felt (from left to right, models b/d)
2 x 3 cm x 10 cm pieces sky blue/light blue (flowers)
3 x 2.5 cm x 10 cm pieces green/light green (leaves)
Other supplies (for each model)
2 x (b, d)/3 x (a, c) 36 cm lengths of 0.55 mm steel wire (flowers)
3 x (b, d)/5 x (a, c) 18 cm lengths of 0.55 mm steel wire (flowers)
Green floral ribbon

Full-size templates on this page.

1 Make the flowers.

G-2 (see p. 36)

1

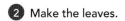

0.5cm

Fold the flower piece in 2, then sew the edge. Notch to 0.5 cm of edge, 0.3 cm apart.

L (see p. 38)

2

Fold the length of wire in 2, then place it on the notched end (★). Apply glue and roll in a spiral.

3

a·c 6cm
b·d 4cm

Glue all the way to the end of the piece. Make 3 flowers (a, c)/2 flowers (b, d).

2 Make the leaves.

E (see p. 35)

Punch 1 hole through the thickness of the felt and insert 1 length of wire. Make 5 components (a, c)/3 components (b, d).

3 Assemble the flower and the leaves.

S (see p. 40)

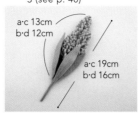

a·c 13cm
b·d 12cm

a·c 19cm
b·d 16cm

Join the flower and the leaves by wrapping them in floral ribbon. Cut excess wire and cover ends with floral ribbon.

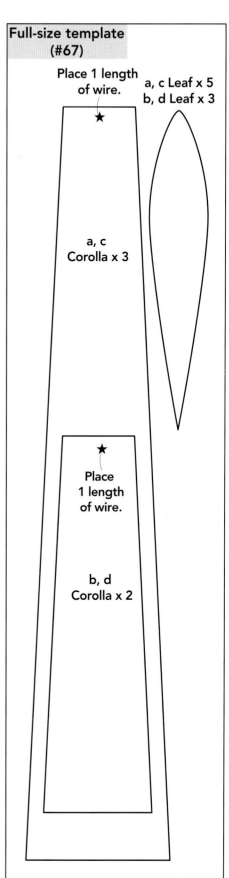

Full-size template (#67)

Place 1 length of wire.
★

a, c Leaf x 5
b, d Leaf x 3

a, c
Corolla x 3

★
Place 1 length of wire.

b, d
Corolla x 2

68. Black Hellebore P. 21

a

b

Supplies

Felt (from left to right, models a/b)
1 x 8 cm x 8 cm piece dark red/light green (corolla)
3 x 3.5 cm x 5.5 cm pieces dark green/green (chalices)
2 x 6.5 cm x 6.5 cm pieces dark green/green (leaves)
1 x 1 cm x 6 cm piece light yellow (A heart)
1 x 2 cm x 4 cm piece light yellow (B heart)
1 x 4 cm x 4 cm piece light green (C heart)

Other supplies (for each model)
1 x 36 cm length of 0.55 mm steel wire (heart)
3 x 18 cm lengths of 0.3 mm steel wire (chalices)
2 x 18 cm lengths of 0.55 mm steel wire (leaves)
Green floral ribbon

Full-size templates p. 91

① Make the heart.
G-1 (see p. 36), H (see p. 36)   K (see p. 37)

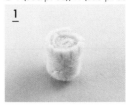

1

Notch the A heart over 0.5 cm, 0.3 cm apart. Roll up and sew bottom in a cross shape.

2

Make a circular support of 0.6 cm in diameter with 1 length of wire. Glue the A heart.

G (see p. 36)

3

Notch the B heart over 1.5 cm, 0.3 cm apart. Sew the unnotched long side. Stitch into the 1st stitch to form a ring.

4

Pull the thread to tighten.

5

Insert the wire from step 1-2 in the centre of the B heart. Apply glue to the side and bottom of the A heart and glue in place.

R (see p. 40)

6

Punch 1 hole in the centre of the C heart, then insert the wire from step 1-5. Apply glue.

7

Glue together.

② Make the flower.
F-1 (see p. 35)

1

Sew the centre of the corolla. Stitch into the 1st stitch.

2

Pull the thread to tighten.

R (see p. 40)

3

Punch 1 hole in the centre of the corolla, then insert the heart wire. Apply glue.

4

Glue together.

③ Make the chalices and the leaves.
E (see p. 35)

chalice   leaf

Punch 1 hole through the thickness of the felt and insert 1 length of wire. Make 3 chalices and 2 leaves.

④ Assemble the flowers, chalices, and leaves.
S (see p. 40)

12cm

17cm

Join the flower and the chalices and wrap in floral ribbon. Join the leaves by wrapping them in floral ribbon. Cut excess wire and cover ends with floral ribbon.

69. Common Poppy P. 21

a

b

Supplies
Felt (from left to right, models a/b)
2 x 6 cm x 6 cm pieces light orange/orange red (corollas)
1 x 2 cm x 4 cm piece light orange/orange red (bud)
1 x 4 cm x 4 cm piece light green (A heart)
1 x 1.3 cm x 3.6 cm piece light green (B heart)
1 x 2.5 cm x 4 cm piece green (chalice)
3 x 5 cm x 7 cm pieces green (leaves)

Full-size templates p. 110

Other supplies (for each model)
1 x 0.2 cm purple bead (heart)
2 x 0.6 cm 0.9 cm beige wooden beads (heart, bud)
1 x 0.3 cm cream/orange bead (bud)
1 x 36 cm length of 0.55 mm steel wire (heart)
1 x 36 cm length of 0.55 mm steel wire (bud)
3 x 18 cm lengths of 0.55 mm steel wire (leaves)
Purple embroidery thread (3740) (heart)
Green floral ribbon

① Make the heart.

C-3 (see p. 34)

G-1 (see p. 36)

1

2

3

4

Embroider 1 double cross stitch with 2 strands at the centre of the A heart.

Punch 2 holes. Thread the round bead onto 1 length of wire and fold the wire it in 2. Insert the wire in the holes.

Thread the wooden bead onto the wire from step 1-2, then glue each petal from the A heart.

Cut 1 edge of the B heart with the notching scissors, then notch. Glue the B heart around the component from step 1-3.

② Make the flower.

M (see p. 38)

R (see p. 40)

1

(wrong side)

2

(right side)

3

4

Sew the corolla using the front stitch. Pull the thread to tighten. Make 2 components.

Punch 1 hole in the centre of the corolla, then insert the heart wire. Glue together.

Apply glue to the bottom of the corolla, then glue the other corolla.

Stagger the petals. The flower is complete.

③ Make the bud.

B-1 (see p. 33), C-1 (see p. 34)

approximately 1 cm

④ Make the leaves.

E (see p. 35)

⑤ Assemble the flower, bud, and leaves.

S (see p. 40)

9cm

17cm

Thread the round bead, followed by the wooden bead, onto 1 length of wire. Glue together. Punch 1 hole in the centre of the bud, then insert the wire. Glue together. Wrap in floral ribbon and bend the stem.

Punch 1 hole through the thickness of the felt and insert 1 length of wire. Make 3 leaves.

Join the flower, bud, and the leaves by wrapping floral ribbon around them. Cut excess wire and cover ends with floral ribbon.

Double cross stitch

5o
2i
3o
4i
1o

5o
7o
6i

8i

o = out, i = in

103

70. Anemone P. 21

a

b

Supplies

Felt (from left to right, models a/b)
1 x 6.5 cm x 6.5 cm piece red/violet (A corolla)
1 x 7.5 cm x 7.5 cm piece red/violet (B corolla)
3 x 6 cm x 6 cm pieces yellow-green/green (leaves)
1 x 0.5 cm x 3 cm piece light yellow (A heart)
1 x 1.5 cm x 3.6 cm piece dark blue (B heart)

Other supplies (for each model)
1 x 36 cm length of 0.55 mm steel wire (flower)
3 x 18 cm length of 0.55 mm steel wire (leaves)
1 x 0.8 cm violet pompom (heart)
Green floral ribbon

Full-size templates p. 83

1 Make the heart.
K (see p. 37)

1

Make a circular support of 0.8 cm in diameter with 1 length of wire. Apply glue and glue the pompom.

G-1 (see p. 36)

2

Notch the A heart over 0.3 cm, 0.3 cm apart.

3

Apply glue to the unnotched side.

4

Glue the A heart around the pompom.

G-1 (see p. 36)

5

Cut 1 long side of the B heart with the notching scissors. Notch, then apply glue to the unnotched side.

6

Glue the B heart around the A heart.

2 Make the flower.
F-1 (see p. 35)

1

Sew the centre of the A corolla. Stitch into the 1st stitch.

2

B corolla   A corolla

Pull the thread to tighten. Make the B corolla in the same manner.

R (see p. 40)

3

Punch 1 hole in the centre of the A corolla, then insert the heart wire. Apply glue.

4

Glue together.

5

Glue the B corolla in the same manner, staggering the petals.

3 Make the leaves.
D (see p. 34)

Apply glue to the bottom of the leaf and attach 1 length of wire. Make 3 leaves.

4 Assemble the flower and the leaves.
S (see p. 40)

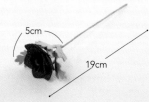

5cm

19cm

Join the flower and the leaves by wrapping floral ribbon around them. Cut excess wire and cover ends with floral ribbon.

71. Japanese Anemone P. 21

 a
 b

Full-size templates on this page.

Supplies
Felt (from left to right, models a/b)
1 x 6 cm x 6 cm piece pink/off-white (corolla)
3 x 3.5 cm x 3.5 cm pieces pink/off-white (bud)
1 x 1 cm x 5 cm piece yellow (heart)
2 x 5.5 cm x 5.5 cm pieces very dark green/
dark green (leaves)

Other supplies (for each model)
3 x 0.3 cm light pink/white beads (buds)
3 x 0.6 cm beige wooden bead (buds)
1 x 0.8 cm green pompom (heart)
1 x 36 cm length of 0.55 mm steel wire (heart)
3 x 36 cm lengths of 0.55 mm steel wire (buds)
2 x 18 cm length of 0.55 mm steel wire (leaves)
Green floral ribbon

① Make the heart.

K (see p. 37)

1

Make a circular support of 0.5 cm in diameter with 1 length of wire. Apply glue and glue the pompom.

G-1 (see p. 36)

2

Notch the heart over 0.5 cm, 0.3 cm apart. Sew the unnotched side and stitch into the 1st stitch. Pull the thread to tighten.

3

Insert wire from step 1-1 through the yellow heart, then glue together.

② Make the flower.

F-1 (see p. 35)

1

Sew the centre of the corolla. Stitch into the 1st stitch, then pull the thread to tighten.

2

Punch 1 hole in the centre of the corolla, then insert the heart wire and glue together. Wrap in floral ribbon.

③ Make the buds.

B-1 (see p. 33)

1

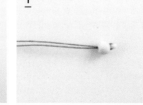

Thread 1 bead onto 1 length of wire, then fold the wire in 2. Thread 1 wooden bead onto both strands of wire. Glue together.

④ Make the leaves.

C-3 (see p. 34)

2

Punch 1 hole in the centre of the bud, then insert the bud wire and glue in place. Wrap in floral ribbon. Make 3 buds.

E (see p. 35)

Punch 1 hole through the thickness of the felt, then insert and glue 1 length of wire. Make 2 leaves.

⑤ Assemble the flower, buds, and leaves.

S (see p. 40)

17cm

8cm

Join the flower, buds, and leaves by wrapping floral ribbon around them. Cut excess wire and cover ends with floral ribbon.

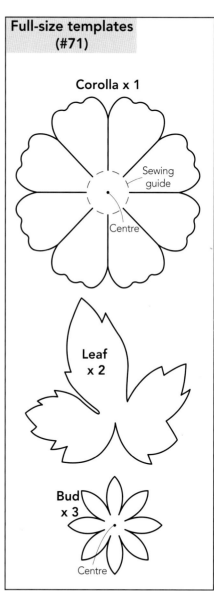

Full-size templates (#71)

Corolla x 1

Sewing guide

Centre

Leaf x 2

Bud x 3

Centre

72. Rhodanthe P. 22

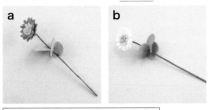

a   b

Full-size templates on this page.

Supplies
Felt (from left to right, models a/b)
2 x 4 cm x 4 cm pieces coral/off-white (corollas)
3 x 3.5 cm x 3.5 cm pieces yellow-green/green (leaves)
1 x 3 cm x 3 cm piece dark yellow (A heart)
1 x 3 cm x 3 cm piece yellow (B heart)

Other supplies (for each model)
1 x 36 cm length of 0.55 mm steel wire (flower)
3 x 18 cm lengths of 0.3 mm steel wire (leaves)
Green floral ribbon

---

1 Make the heart.

J (see p. 37)   R (see p. 40)

1   2   3

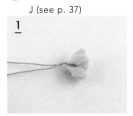      

Fold the A heart twice, then attach 1 length of wire, folded in 2. Fold wire 2 or 3 times at the bottom of the heart.

Punch 1 hole in the centre of the B heart, then insert the wire from step 1-1. Apply glue.

Glue together.

2 Make the flower.

R (see p. 40)

Punch 1 hole in the centre of the corolla, then insert the heart wire and glue together. Glue another corolla, staggering the petals.

3 Make the leaves.

E (see p. 35)

Punch 1 hole through the thickness of the felt, then insert and glue 1 length of wire. Make 3 leaves.

4 Assemble the flower and the leaves.

S (see p. 40)

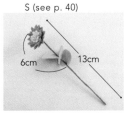

6cm   13cm

Join the flower and the leaves by wrapping floral ribbon around them. Cut excess wire and cover ends with floral ribbon.

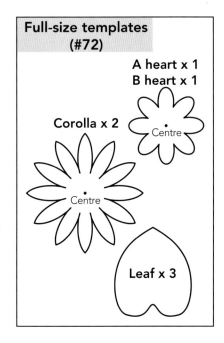

Full-size templates (#72)

A heart x 1
B heart x 1

Corolla x 2

Centre

Centre

Leaf x 3

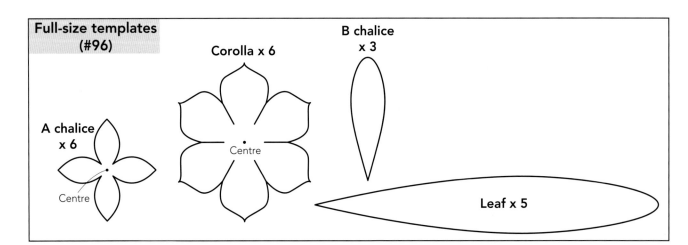

Full-size templates (#96)

B chalice x 3

Corolla x 6

Centre

A chalice x 6

Centre

Leaf x 5

73. Frost Aster P. 22

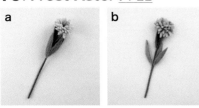
a   b

Supplies
Felt (from left to right, models a/b)
4 x 4 cm x 4 cm pieces pink/purple (corollas)
1 x 3.5 cm x 3.5 cm piece green (heart)
5 x 1.5 cm x 4.5 cm pieces dark green (leaves)

Other supplies (for each model)
4 x 36 cm lengths of 0.3 mm steel wire (corollas)
1 x 36 cm length of 0.3 mm steel wire (heart)
5 x 18 cm length of 0.3 mm steel wire (leaves)
1 x 0.6 cm beige wooden bead (heart)
Green floral ribbon

Full-size templates below.

1 Make the heart.
B-3 (see p. 33), C-3 (see p. 34)

Thread the bead onto a length of wire and twist the wire 2 or 3 times at the bottom of the bead. Punch 1 hole in the centre of the heart, then insert the wire and glue together.

2 Make the flower.
J (see p. 37)

1

Fold the corolla twice, then attach 1 length of wire, folded in 2. Twist the wire 2 or 3 times at the bottom of the corolla. Make 4 components.

2

Assemble the corollas around the heart.

3

Twist the wires 2 or 3 times at the bottom of the flower.

3 Make the leaves.
E (see p. 35)

Punch 1 hole through the thickness of the felt, then insert and glue 1 length of wire. Make 5 leaves.

4 Assemble the flower and the leaves.
S (see p. 40)

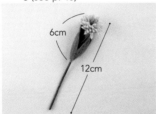
6cm
12cm

Join the flower and the leaves by wrapping floral ribbon around them. Cut excess wire and cover ends with floral ribbon.

Full-size templates (#100)

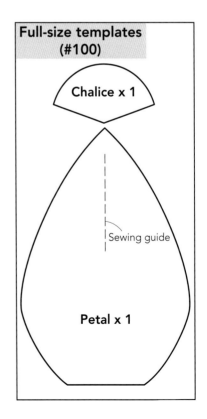
Chalice x 1
Sewing guide
Petal x 1

Full-size templates (#73)

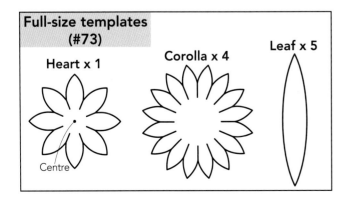
Heart x 1
Centre
Corolla x 4
Leaf x 5

74. Cornflower P. 22

Supplies

Felt

6 x 3 cm x 3 cm pieces purple (hearts)

12 x 3 cm x 4 cm pieces blue (petals)

3 x 2 cm x 5 cm pieces yellow-green (leaves)

Other supplies

2 x 36 cm lengths of 0.3 mm steel wire (hearts)

12 x 18 cm lengths of 0.3 mm steel wire (petals)

3 x 18 cm lengths of 0.3 mm steel wire (leaves)

Green floral ribbon

Full-size templates below.

1 Make the heart.

J (see p. 37), R (see p. 40)

1 Fold the heart twice, then attach 1 length of wire, folded in 2. Twist the wire 2 or 3 times at the bottom of the heart. Punch 1 hole in the centre of another heart, insert the wire and glue together.

2 Glue another heart in the same manner.

2 Make the flowers.

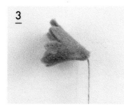

1 Apply glue to the bottom of the petal, then glue 1 length of wire.

2 Pinch the bottom of the petal and hold in place with a clamp. Leave to dry.

3 Bend the wire at a 90-degree angle at the base of the petal. Make 6 petals.

4 Assemble the petals around the heart.

5 Twist the wires 2 or 3 times at the bottom of the flower. Make 2 flowers.

3 Make the leaves.

E (see p. 35)

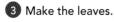

Punch 1 hole through the thickness of the felt, then insert and glue 1 length of wire. Make 3 leaves.

4 Assemble the flower and the leaves.

S (see p. 40)

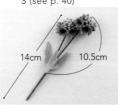

14cm   10.5cm

Join the flower and the leaves by wrapping floral ribbon around them. Cut excess wire and cover ends with floral ribbon.

Full-size templates (#95)

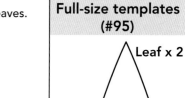

Leaf x 2

Cut   Cut

B corolla x 3

Sewing guide   Centre

C corolla x 7

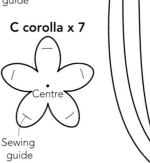

Centre

Sewing guide

A corolla x 3

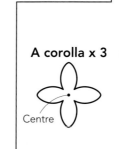

Centre

Full-size templates (#74)

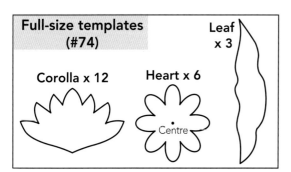

Leaf x 3

Corolla x 12

Heart x 6

Centre

75. Marigold P. 22

Full-size templates p. 110.

Supplies

Felt

1 x 3 cm x 3 cm piece yellow (A heart)
1 x 4 cm x 4 cm piece yellow (B heart)
1 x 4.5 cm x 4.5 cm piece dark orange (A corolla)
1 x 4.5 cm x 4.5 cm piece yellow (B corolla)
1 x 5.5 cm x 5.5 cm piece dark orange (C corolla)
1 x 5.5 cm x 5.5 cm piece yellow (D corolla)
2 x 3 cm x 4 cm pieces green (A leaves)
4 x 2 cm x 3.5 cm pieces green (B leaves)

Other supplies

1 x 36 cm length of 0.55 mm steel wire (flower)
6 x 18 cm lengths of 0.3 mm steel wire (leaves)
Green floral ribbon

1 Make the heart.

J (see p. 37)

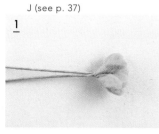

1

Fold the A heart twice, then attach 1 length of wire, folded in 2. Twist the wire 2 or 3 times at the bottom of the heart.

F-1 (see p. 35)

2

Sew the centre of the B heart. Stitch into the 1st stitch.

3

Pull the thread to tighten.

R (see p. 40)

4

Punch 1 hole in the centre of the B heart, then insert the wire from step 1-1. Apply glue.

2 Make the flower.

5

Glue together.

1

A corolla   B corolla

Prepare 1 A corolla and 1 B corolla.

F-2 (see p. 35)

2

Overlay the corollas and sew the centre. Stitch into the 1st stitch.

3

Pull the thread to tighten.

R (see p. 40)

4

Punch 1 hole in the centre of the corollas, then insert the heart wire.

5

Apply glue and glue together.

6

Overlay the C and D corollas and sew the centre. Stitch into the 1st stitch.

R (see p. 40)

7

Pull the thread to tighten. Punch 1 hole in the centre, then insert the wire from step 2-5.

Continued p. 110.

3 Make the leaves.

E (see p. 35)

<u>1</u> A leaf, B leaf, B leaf

Punch 1 hole through the thickness of the felt, then insert and glue 1 length of wire. Make 1 A leaf and 2 B leaves.

<u>2</u>

Assemble the 3 leaves from step 3-1, then wrap in floral ribbon. Make 2 identical components.

4 Assemble the flower and the leaves.

S (see p. 40)

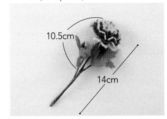

10.5cm, 14cm

Join the flower and the leaves by wrapping floral ribbon around them. Cut excess wire and cover ends with floral ribbon.

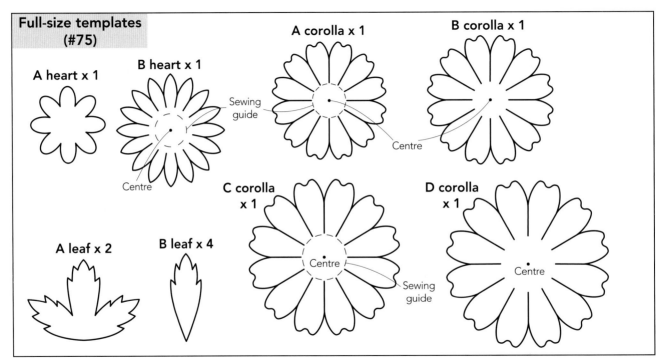

Full-size templates (#75)

A heart x 1
B heart x 1 — Sewing guide, Centre
A corolla x 1 — Centre
B corolla x 1
C corolla x 1 — Centre, Sewing guide
D corolla x 1 — Centre
A leaf x 2
B leaf x 4

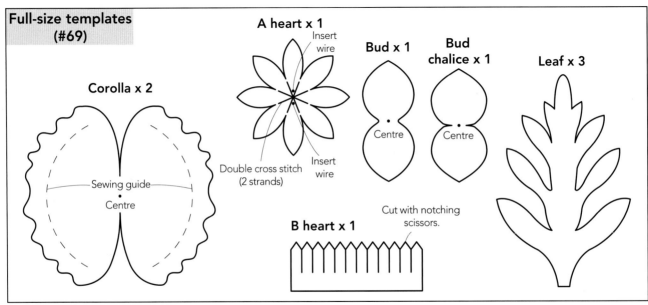

Full-size templates (#69)

Corolla x 2 — Sewing guide, Centre
A heart x 1 — Insert wire, Insert wire, Double cross stitch (2 strands)
Bud x 1 — Centre
Bud chalice x 1 — Centre
Leaf x 3
B heart x 1 — Cut with notching scissors.

76. Strawflower P. 22

Full-size templates below.

Supplies (from left to right: models a/b)
Felt
2 x 4 cm x 4 cm pieces yellow (A corollas)
2 x 4.5 cm x 4.5 cm pieces orange/pink (B corollas)
2 x 5 cm x 5 cm pieces dark orange/dark pink (C corollas)
3 x 2 cm x 4.5 cm pieces yellow-green/light green (leaves)

Other supplies (for each model)
1 x 36 cm length of 0.45 mm steel wire (flower)
3 x 18 cm lengths of 0.3 mm steel wire (leaves)
1 x 0.8 cm beige wooden bead (heart)
Green floral ribbon

1 Make the heart.

B-3 (see p. 33)

1

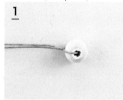

Thread the bead onto 1 length of wire, then twist the wire 2 or 3 times at the bottom of the bead.

C-3 (see p. 34)

2

Punch 1 hole in the centre of the A corolla, then insert the heart wire. Apply glue to every other petal.

3

Glue the 4 petals to the bead.

4

Apply glue to the 4 remaining petals, then glue in place.

R (see p. 40)

5

Punch 1 hole in the centre of another A corolla, then insert the wire from step 1-4. Apply glue.

6

Glue together.

2 Make the flower.

R (see p. 40)

1

Punch 1 hole in the centre of the B corolla, then insert the wire from step 1-6 and glue together. Glue another B corolla in the same manner, staggering the petals.

2

Punch 1 hole in the centre of the C corolla, then insert the wire from step 2-1. Glue another C corolla in the same manner, staggering the petals.

3 Make the leaves.

E (see p. 35)

Punch 1 hole through the thickness of the felt, then insert and glue 1 length of wire. Make 3 leaves.

4 Assemble the flower and the leaves.

S (see p. 40)

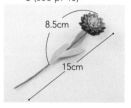

Join the flower and the leaves by wrapping floral ribbon around them. Cut excess wire and cover ends with floral ribbon.

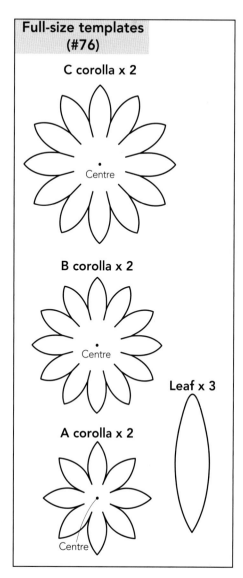

Full-size templates (#76)

C corolla x 2

Centre

B corolla x 2

Centre

A corolla x 2

Centre

Leaf x 3

77. African Daisy P. 22

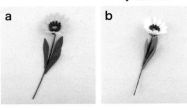

a   b

Full-size templates below.

Supplies (from left to right: models a/b)
Felt
1 x 7 cm x 7 cm piece yellow/off-white (corolla)
1 x 4 cm x 4 cm piece dark green/green (chalice)
3 x 2 cm x 6 cm pieces dark green/green (leaves)
1 x 0.5 cm x 7 cm piece dark yellow (A heart)
1 x 0.9 cm x 3.5 cm piece dark orange (B heart)
1 x 1.2 cm x 4.2 cm piece maroon (C heart)

Other supplies
1 x 36 cm length of 0.55 mm steel wire (heart)
3 x 18 cm lengths of 0.3 mm steel wire (leaves)
Green floral ribbon

① Make the heart.

H (see p. 36)   G-1 (see p. 36)   K (see p. 37)

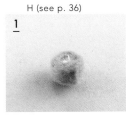   

1 Roll up the A heart then sew the bottom in a cross shape.

2 Notch 1 long side of the B heart over 0.5 cm, 0.3 cm apart. Wrap it around the A heart and sew the bottom in a cross shape.

3 Cut 1 long side of the C heart with the notching scissors, then notch. Wrap it around the B heart.

4 Make a circular support with 1 length of wire, then glue the heart.

② Make the flower.

R (see p. 40)

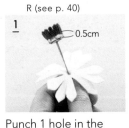 

1 Punch 1 hole in the centre of the corolla, then insert the heart wire. Apply glue to the side and bottom of the heart.

0.5cm

2 Glue together.

③ Glue the chalice.

R (see p. 40)

1 Punch 1 hole in the centre of the chalice, then insert the flower wire. Apply glue.

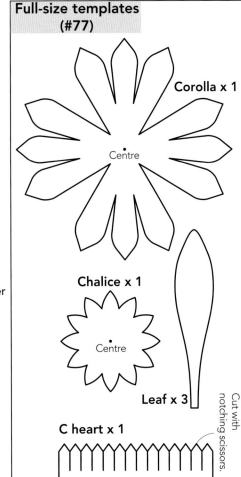

Full-size templates (#77)

Corolla x 1

Centre

Chalice x 1

Centre

Leaf x 3

Cut with notching scissors.

C heart x 1

④ Make the leaves.

E (see p. 35)

2 Glue the chalice to the side and bottom of the flower.

Punch 1 hole through the thickness of the felt, then insert and glue 1 length of wire. Make 3 leaves.

⑤ Assemble the flower and the leaves.

S (see p. 40)

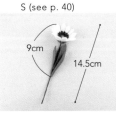

9cm   14.5cm

Join the flower and the leaves by wrapping floral ribbon around them. Cut excess wire and cover ends with floral ribbon.

78. Zinnia P. 23

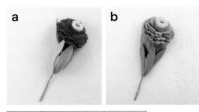

a   b

Full-size templates p. 118.

Supplies (from left to right: models a/b)

Felt

1 x 3.5 cm x 3.5 cm piece red/pink (A corolla)
2 x 5 cm x 5 cm pieces red/pink (B corollas)
2 x 6 cm x 6 cm pieces red/pink (C corollas)
2 x 6 cm x 6 cm pieces red/pink (D corollas)
1 x 0.8 cm x 5 cm piece dark maroon/dark red (A heart)
1 x 1.2 cm x 7.5 cm piece yellow (B heart)
5 x 2 cm x 6 cm pieces yellow-green/green (leaves)

Other supplies (for each model)

2 x 36 cm lengths of 0.3 mm steel wire (corollas)
1 x 36 cm length of 0.45 mm steel wire (heart)
5 x 18 cm lengths of 0.3 mm steel wire (leaves)
Green floral ribbon

1 Make the heart.

H (see p. 36)

1

Notch the A heart over 0.5 cm, 0.3 cm apart. Roll it up, then sew the bottom in a cross shape to secure.

2

Notch the B heart over 0.7 cm, 0.3 cm apart. Apply glue and wrap it around the A heart.

K (see p. 37)

3

Make a circular support of 0.6 cm in diameter with 1 length of wire, then glue to the heart from step 1-2.

2 Make the flower.

R (see p. 40)

1

Punch 1 hole in the centre of the A corolla, then insert the heart wire and glue together.

J (see p. 37)

2

Fold the B corolla in 2, then place the length of wire in the groove of the folded piece. Twist the wire 2 or 3 times at the bottom of the corolla. Make 2 components and place them around the heart.

3

Twist the wires 2 or 3 times at the bottom of the corolla.

4

Punch 1 hole in the centre of the C corolla, then insert the wire from step 2-3. Glue 2 C corollas, then 2 D corollas.

3 Make the leaves.

E (see p. 35)

Punch 1 hole through the thickness of the felt, then insert and glue 1 length of wire. Make 5 components.

4 Assemble the flower and the leaves.

S (see p. 40)

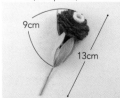

9cm   13cm

Join the flower and the leaves by wrapping floral ribbon around them. Cut excess wire and cover ends with floral ribbon.

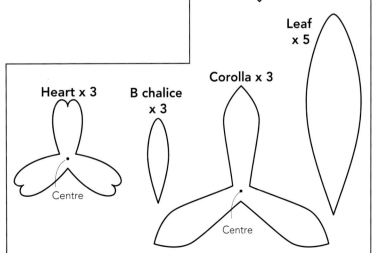

Full-size templates (#94)

A chalice x 3

Centre

Leaf x 5

Heart x 3

Centre

B chalice x 3

Corolla x 3

Centre

79. Chrysanthemum P. 24

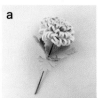 a
 b

Full-size templates below.

Supplies (from left to right: models a/b)
Felt
1 x 2.5 cm x 10 cm piece yellow/pink (A corolla)
1 x 5 cm x 7 cm piece yellow/pink (B corolla)
1 x 6 cm x 9 cm piece light yellow/light pink (C corolla)
1 x 7 cm x 11 cm piece light yellow/light pink (D corolla)
1 x 5.5 cm x 5.5 cm piece yellow-green/green (chalice)
3 x 5 cm x 7 cm pieces yellow-green/green (leaves)

Other supplies (for each model)
1 x 36 cm length of 0.8 mm steel wire (flower)
3 x 18 cm lengths of 0.45 mm steel wire (leaves)
Green floral ribbon

1 Make the A corolla.

G-2 (see p. 36)

1 Fold the A corolla in 2, then sew 1 long side. Notch over 0.7 cm, 0.3 cm apart. Sew the unnotched side and stitch into the first stitch.

2 Pull the thread to tighten.

3 Sew the bottom in a cross shape (see p. 36).

K (see p. 37)

4 Make a circular support of 1.3 cm in diameter with 1 length of wire, then glue the A corolla.

2 Make the B to D corollas.

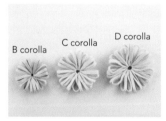

B corolla   C corolla   D corolla

Fold each piece in 2, then notch over 2 cm (B)/2.5 cm (C)/3 cm (D), 0.3 cm apart. Sew and tighten in the same manner as the A corolla.

3 Make the flower.

1 Insert the wire from the A corolla into the centre of the B corolla and glue together.

2 Glue the C corolla, then the D corolla in the same manner.

4 Glue the chalice.

R (see p. 40)

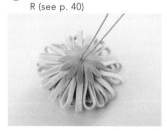

Punch 1 hole in the centre of the chalice, then insert the flower wire and glue together.

5 Make the leaves.

E (see p. 35)

Punch 1 hole through the thickness of the felt, then insert and glue 1 length of wire. Make 3 leaves.

6 Assemble the flower and the leaves.

S (see p. 40)

8cm
16cm

Join the flower and the leaves by wrapping floral ribbon around them. Cut excess wire and cover ends with floral ribbon.

Full-size template (#79)

Chalice x 1

Centre

Leaf x 3

81. Aster P. 24

a

b

Full-size templates p. 128.

Supplies (from left to right: models a/b)
Felt
4 x 5.5 cm x 5.5 cm pieces pink/violet (A corollas)
2 x 5.5 cm x 5.5 cm pieces coral/purple (B corollas)
2 x 7 cm x 7 cm pieces dark green/yellow-green (chalices)
3 x 1.5 cm x 5.5 cm pieces dark green/yellow-green (leaves)
1x 4 cm x 4 cm piece yellow (heart)

Other supplies (for each model)
4 x 36 cm lengths of 0.3 mm steel wire (corollas)
1 x 36 cm length of 0.3 mm steel wire (heart)
2 x 36 cm lengths of 0.3 mm steel wire (chalices)
3x 18 cm lengths of 0.3 mm steel wire (leaves)
Green floral ribbon

1 Make the flower.

J (see p. 37)

1

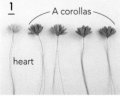
A corollas
heart

Fold the heart twice, then attach 1 length of wire, folded in 2. Twist the wire 2 or 3 times. Make 4 A corollas in the same manner.

2

Assemble the 4 A corollas around the heart, then twist the wires 2 or 3 times at the bottom of the corollas.

R (see p. 40)

3

Punch a hole in the centre of the B corolla, then insert the wire from step 1-2 and glue together. Glue another B corolla, staggering the petals.

2 Secure the chalices.

1

Fold the chalice in 2 and punch 1 hole as indicated.

2

Insert 1 length of wire in the hole, then twist it 2 or 3 times close to the chalice. Make 2 identical components.

3

Place both chalices under the flower, B side on top.

4

Twist the wires.

3 Make the leaves.

E (see p. 35)

Punch 1 hole through the thickness of the felt, then insert and glue 1 length of wire. Make 3 leaves.

4 Assemble the flower and the leaves.

S (see p. 40)

9cm
15cm

Join the flower and the leaves by wrapping floral ribbon around them. Cut excess wire and cover ends with floral ribbon.

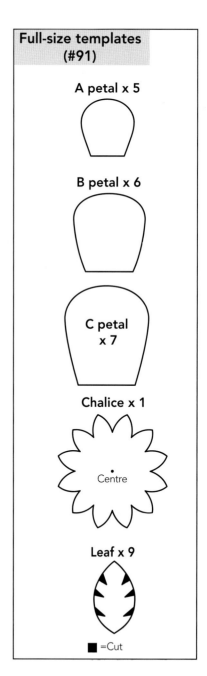

Full-size templates (#91)

A petal x 5

B petal x 6

C petal x 7

Chalice x 1

Centre

Leaf x 9

■ =Cut

115

80. Dhalia P. 24

a   b

Full-size templates p. 117.

Supplies (from left to right: models a/b)
Felt
2 x 4 cm x 4 cm pieces light orange/green (A corollas)
2 x 5.5 cm x 5.5 cm pieces light orange/green (B corollas)
2 x 7 cm x 7 cm pieces light pink/moss green (C corollas)
1 x 8 cm x 8 cm piece light pink/moss green (D corolla)
1 x 8 cm x 8 cm piece light yellow/light green (E corolla)
3 x 9 cm x 9 cm pieces light yellow/light green (F corollas)
2 x 3.5 cm x 4.5 cm pieces green/dark green (A leaves)
4 x 2.5 cm x 3.5 cm pieces green/dark green (B leaves)
4 x 3 cm x 4.5 cm pieces green/dark green (C leaves)

Other supplies (for each model)
1 x 0.3 cm light yellow/mat green bead (heart)
1 x 0.6 cm x 0.9 cm beige wooden bead (heart)
1 x 36 cm length of 0.8 mm steel wire (heart)
10 x 18 cm lengths of 0.3 mm steel wire (leaves)
Green floral ribbon

1 Make the heart.

B-1 (see p. 33)

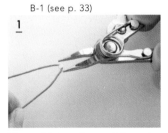

C-3 (see p. 34)

1 Thread 1 bead onto 1 length of wire and fold in 2.

2 Thread wooden bead onto 2 strands of wire and glue together.

3 Punch 1 hole in the centre of the A corolla, then insert the wire from step 1-2 and glue together.

4 Glue another A corolla in the same manner.

2 Make the flower.

F corollas

D corolla   E corolla

1 Prepare 3 F corollas. Empty a circle in the centre of 2 F corollas, then apply glue around the opening.

2 Overlay the 2 emptied corollas on top of the 3rd F corolla, staggering the petals.

3 Press on the centre to glue together and to add texture.

4 Prepare 1 D corolla and 1 E corolla. Empty their centre, then apply glue around the opening.

C corollas

B corollas

5 Overlay the E corolla, followed by the D corolla onto the component from step 2-3, staggering the petals. Press on the centre to add texture.

6 Empty the centres of the 2 C corollas and apply glue.

7 Overlay the C corollas onto the component from step 2-5, staggering the petals. Press on the centre to add texture.

8 Empty the centres of the 2 B corollas and apply glue.

Continued p. 117

9

Overlay the B corollas, staggering the petals, then press on the centre.

10

The corollas are all glued.

R (see p. 40)

11

Punch a hole in the centre of the component from step 2-10, then insert the heart wire. Apply glue.

12

Glue together.

③ Make the leaves.

E (see p. 35)

1

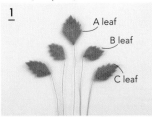

Punch 1 hole through the thickness of the felt, then insert and glue 1 length of wire. Make 1 A leaf, 2 B leaves   and 2 C leaves.

2

Assemble 1 A leaf, 2 B leaves, then 2 C leaves by wrapping them in floral ribbon. Make 2 identical pieces.

④ Assemble the flower and the leaves.

S (see p. 40)

Join the flower and the leaves by wrapping floral ribbon around them. Cut excess wire and cover ends with floral ribbon.

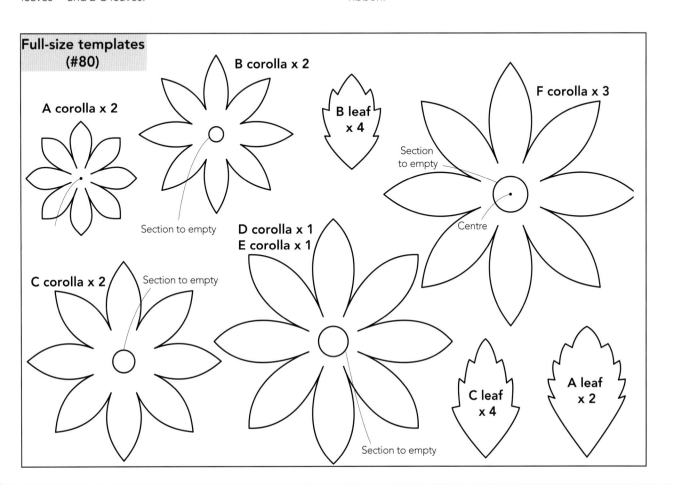

Full-size templates (#80)

A corolla x 2

B corolla x 2

B leaf x 4

F corolla x 3

Section to empty

Centre

Section to empty

C corolla x 2

Section to empty

D corolla x 1
E corolla x 1

C leaf x 4

A leaf x 2

Section to empty

82. Chinese Aster P. 24

a b

Supplies (from left to right: models a/b)
Felt
1 x 5 cm x 5 cm piece dark orange/yellow-green (A corolla)
6 x 5 cm x 5 cm pieces red/light green (B corollas)
3 x 3 cm x 5 cm pieces dark green/green (leaves)

Other supplies (for each model)
5 x 36 cm lengths of 0.3 mm steel wire (flowers)
3 x 18 cm lengths of 0.3 mm steel wire (leaves)
Green floral ribbon

Full-size templates on this page.

1 Make the flower.
J (see p. 37)

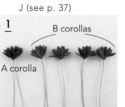
1
B corollas
A corolla

Fold the A corolla twice, then attach 1 length of wire, folded in 2. Twist the wire 2 or 3 times at the bottom of the corolla. Make 4 B corollas in the same manner.

2

Assemble the 4 B corollas around the A corolla.

3

Twist the wires 2 or 3 times at the bottom of the corolla.

R (see p. 40)

4

Punch 1 hole in the centre of a B corolla, then insert the wire from step 1-3 and glue together. Glue another B corolla, staggering the petals.

2 Make the leaves.
E (see p. 35)

Punch 1 hole through the thickness of the felt, then insert and glue 1 length of wire. Make 3 leaves.

3 Assemble the flower and the leaves.
S (see p. 40)

6cm
14cm

Join the flower and the leaves by wrapping floral ribbon around them. Cut excess wire and cover ends with floral ribbon.

Full-size template (#82)
A corolla x 1
B corolla x 6
Centre
Leaf x 3

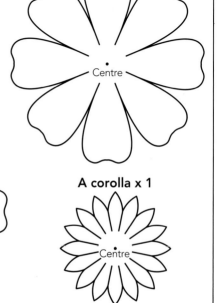

Full-size templates (#78)
B corolla x 2

Leaf x 5

C corolla x 2
Centre

D corolla x 2
Centre

A corolla x 1
Centre

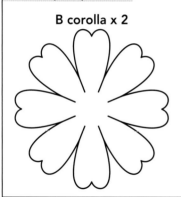

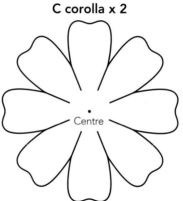

83. Pot Marigold P. 24

Supplies
Felt
1 x 4 cm x 4 cm piece orange (A corolla)
4 x 6 cm x 6 cm pieces orange (B corollas)
2 x 6.5 cm x 6.5 cm pieces orange (C corollas)
1 x 3 cm x 3 cm piece maroon (A heart)
1 x 3 cm x 3 cm piece dark orange (B heart)
7 x 3 cm x 7 cm pieces green (leaves)

Full-size templates on p. 78.

Other supplies
4 x 36 cm lengths of 0.3 mm steel wire (corollas)
1 x 36 cm length of 0.45 mm steel wire (heart)
7 x 18 cm lengths of 0.3 mm steel wire (leaves)
Green floral ribbon

1 Make the heart.

J (see p. 37)

1

Fold the A heart twice, then attach 1 length of wire, folded in 2. Twist the wire 2 or 3 times at the bottom of the heart.

R (see p. 40)

2

Punch 1 hole in the centre of the B heart, then insert wire from step 1-1 and glue together.

2 Make the flower.

R (see p. 40)

1

Punch 1 hole in the centre of the A corolla, then insert the heart wire and apply glue.

2

Glue together.

J (see p. 37)

3

Fold the B corolla twice, then attach 1 length of wire, folded in 2. Twist the wire 2 or 3 times at the bottom of the corolla. Make 4 identical components.

4

Assemble the 4 B corollas around the component from step 2-2.

5

Twist the wires 2 or 3 times at the bottom of the corolla.

R (see p. 40)

6

Punch 1 hole in the centre of the C corolla, then insert the wire from step 2-5 and glue together.

7

Glue another C corolla in the same manner, staggering the petals.

3 Make the leaves.

E (see p. 35)

Punch 1 hole through the thickness of the felt, then insert and glue 1 length of wire. Make 7 leaves.

4 Assemble the flower and the leaves.

S (see p. 40)

10cm

14cm

Join the flower and the leaves by wrapping floral ribbon around them. Cut excess wire and cover ends with floral ribbon.

84. Lotus P. 25

a   b

Full-size templates on p. 121.

Supplies (from left to right: models a/b)
Felt
2 x 8 cm x 8 cm pieces dark pink/blue (A corolla)
2 x 9 cm x 9 cm pieces pink/light blue (B corolla)
3 x 5 cm x 5 cm pieces yellow-green/green (leaves)
1 x 1 cm x 8.5 cm piece yellow (A heart)
1 x 1.3 cm x 4.2 cm piece light yellow (B heart)
1 x 1.7 cm x 10.2 cm piece light yellow (C heart)

Other supplies (for each model)
1 x 36 cm length of 0.8 mm steel wire (flower)
3 x 18 cm lengths of 0.55 mm steel wire (leaves)
Green floral ribbon

1 Make the heart.
H (see p. 36)   G-1 (see p. 36)

1 Roll up the A heart.

2 Sew the bottom in a cross shape.

3 Cut 1 long side of the B heart with the notching scissors, then notch. Roll it around the A heart, then sew the bottom in a cross shape.

4 Cut 1 long side of the C heart with the notching scissors, then notch. Roll it around the B heart, then sew the bottom in a cross shape.

2 Make the flower.
F-1 (see p. 35)

1 Sew the centre of the A corolla. Stitch into the 1st stitch.

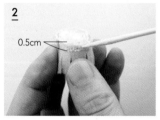

2 0.5cm Apply glue to the side and bottom of the heart.

3 Glue the heart to the centre of the A corolla.

4 Pull the thread to lift the petals.

5 Apply glue to the side and bottom of the component from step 2-4.

6 Glue the component from step 2-5 onto another A corolla, staggering the petals. Pull the thread to lift the petals.

7 Apply glue to the bottom of the A corolla, then glue it in the centre of the B corolla, staggering the petals.

8 Place the component in a small container, such as an egg cup, and leave to dry.

Continued p. 121.

K (see p. 37), R (see p. 40)

9

Make a circular support of 1.8 cm in diameter with 1 length of wire. Punch 1 hole in the centre of the B corolla, then insert the wire.

10

Apply glue around the support, then glue the flower from step 2-8, staggering the petals.

11

Lift the petals, then pin in place and leave to dry.

12

Gently curve the ends of the petals outward.

3 Make the leaves.

E (see p. 35)

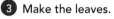

1

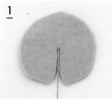

Punch 1 hole through the thickness of the felt, then insert and glue 1 length of wire.

2

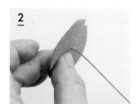

Bend the stem at a 90-degree angle close to the leaf. Make 3 leaves.

4 Assemble the flower and the leaves.

S (see p. 40)

10cm

16cm

Join the flower and the leaves by wrapping floral ribbon around them. Cut excess wire and cover ends with floral ribbon.

C heart x 1

Cut with notching scissors.

B heart x 1

Cut with notching scissors.

Full-size template (#84)

Leaf x 3

A corolla x 2

Sewing guide

B corolla x 2

Centre

85. Leather Flower P. 25

a

b

Full-size templates on p. 100.

Supplies (from left to right: models a/b)

Felt

1 x 8 cm x 8 cm piece dark blue/purple (corolla)
1 x 5.5 cm x 5.5 cm piece dark blue/purple (bud)
3 x 2.5 cm x 4 cm pieces dark green/very dark green (leaves)
1 x 4 cm x 4 cm piece light yellow (A heart)
1 x 1.5 cm x 4.8 cm piece light yellow (B heart)

Other supplies (for each model)

1 x 36 cm length of 0.55 mm steel wire (heart)
1 x 36 cm length of 0.5 mm steel wire (bud)
2 x 18 cm lengths of 0.55 mm steel wire (tendrils)
3 x 18 cm lengths of 0.55 mm steel wire (leaves)
1 x 0.3 cm light green bead (heart)
1 x 0.6 cm x 0.9 cm beige wooden bead (heart)
1 x 0.3 cm light green bead (bud)
1 x 0.8 cm x 1 cm beige wooden bead (bud)
Green floral ribbon

① Make the heart.

B-2 (see p. 33)

1

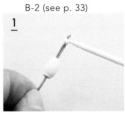

Make the heart.

C-3 (see p. 34)

2

Thread 1 bead onto 1 length of wire, then fold wire in 2. Twist the wire 2 or 3 times at the bottom of the bead. Thread the wooden bead onto the 2 strands of wire, then glue together.

3

Apply glue to the remaining petals and glue them in place.

G-1 (see p. 36)

4

Cut 1 long side of the B heart with the notching scissors, then notch. Sew the unnotched long side and make a ring.

5

Pull the thread to tighten.

6

Insert the wire from step 1-3 and glue together.

② Make the flower.

1

(wrong side)

Fold the bottom of the petal in 2, then stitch 2 or 3 times. Secure with a stop knot.

2

(wrong side)

Sew the remaining petals in the same manner.

R (see p. 40)

3

Punch 1 hole in the centre of the corolla, then insert the heart wire and glue together. Wrap in floral ribbon.

③ Make the bud.

Make the bud following steps 1-1 to 3. Wrap in floral ribbon.

④ Make the leaves.

E (see p. 35)

Punch 1 hole through the thickness of the felt, then insert and glue 1 length of wire. Make 3 leaves.

⑤ Make the tendrils.

1

Wrap the floral ribbon around the length of wire.

2

Wrap the wire around a punch. Make 2 tendrils.

⑥ Assemble the flower, bud, tendrils, and leaves.

S (see p. 40)

11cm

16cm

Join the flower, bud, tendrils. and leaves by wrapping floral ribbon around them. Cut excess wire and cover ends with floral ribbon.

122

86. Poinsettia P. 25

Supplies
Felt
8 x 2 cm x 3 cm pieces red (A petals)
8 x 3 cm x 5 cm pieces red (B petals)
5 x 3.5 cm x 3.5 cm pieces light green (hearts)
5 x 3 cm x 5 cm pieces green (leaves)

Full-size templates below.

Other supplies
5 x 0.3 cm red beads (hearts)
5 x 0.6 cm x 0.9 cm wooden beads (hearts)
5 x 36 cm lengths of 0.3 mm steel wire (hearts)
16 x 18 cm lengths of 0.3 mm steel wire (petals)
5 x 18 cm lengths of 0.3 mm steel wire (leaves)
Green floral ribbon

1 Make the heart.
B-2 (see p. 33), C-1 (see p. 34)

1

Thread 1 wooden bead onto 1 length of wire, then twist the wire 2 or 3 times at the bottom of the bead. Glue together. Punch 1 hole in the centre of the heart, then insert the wire. Glue together. Make 5 hearts.

2

Assemble the 5 hearts and wrap them in floral ribbon.

2 Make the petals.
E (see p. 35)

1

Punch 1 hole through the thickness of the petal, then insert and glue 1 length of wire. Fold the petal in 2 and bend slightly.

2

Hold the petal with a clamp.

3

A petals   B petals

Make 8 A petals and 8 B petals.

3 Make the flower.

1

Assemble 8 A petals around the heart. Wrap in floral ribbon.

2

Assemble 8 B petals around the component from step 3-1. Wrap in floral ribbon.

4 Make the leaves.
E (see p. 35)

Punch 1 hole through the thickness of the felt, then insert and glue 1 length of wire. Bend the stem lightly and hold with a clamp. Make 5 leaves.

5 Assemble the flower and the leaves.
S (see p. 40)

8.5cm
14cm

Join the flower and the leaves by wrapping floral ribbon around them. Cut excess wire and cover ends with floral ribbon.

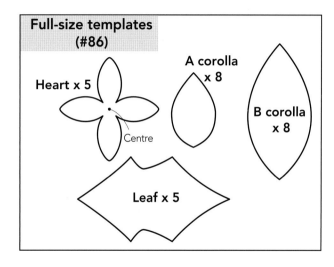

Full-size templates (#86)

Heart x 5
Centre

A corolla x 8

B corolla x 8

Leaf x 5

87. Cyclamen Persicum P. 25

Full-size templates on p. 87.

Supplies

Felt

3 x 11 cm x 11 cm pieces red (corollas)

5 x 5 cm x 5 cm pieces dark green (leaves)

Other supplies

3 x 36 cm lengths of 0.45 mm steel wire (flowers)

5 x 18 cm lengths of 0.3 mm steel wire (leaves)

1 x 10 cm length of 0.3 mm steel wire (to attach)

3 x 0.3 cm yellow beads (hearts)

3 x 0.6 cm x 0.9 cm beige wooden beads (hearts)

Green floral ribbon

① Make the flowers.

B-1 (see p. 33)   R (see p. 40)

1

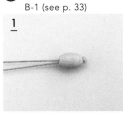

Thread 1 bead onto 1 length of wire, then fold the wire in 2. Thread a wooden bead onto the 2 strands, then glue together.

2

Punch 1 hole in the centre of the corolla, then insert the heart wire. Apply glue to the wooden bead.

3

Lift the petals and glue them to the wooden bead.

4

Wrap in floral ribbon.

5

approximately 0.5 cm

Apply glue 0.5 cm from the bottom of the flower.

6

Fold the petals down and attach with the length of wire and leave to dry.

7

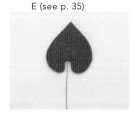

Remove the length of wire and bend the stem. Make 3 flowers.

② Make the leaves.

E (see p. 35)

Punch 1 hole through the thickness of the felt, then insert and glue 1 length of wire. Make 5 leaves.

③ Assemble the flowers and the leaves.

S (see p. 40)

8cm   12cm

Join the flowers and the leaves by wrapping floral ribbon around them. Cut excess wire and cover ends with floral ribbon.

Full-size templates (#88)

Heart x 1

Chalice x 1

• Centre

A corolla x 3

B corolla x 5

Leaf x 8

■ = Cut.

89. Great Maiden's Blush P. 27

Full-size templates on p. 71.

Supplies

Felt

1 x 4 cm x 4 cm piece light orange (A heart)
1 x 5 cm x 5 cm piece light orange (B heart)
1 x 6 cm x 6 cm piece light orange (C heart)
4 x 4.5 cm x 4.5 cm pieces light orange (A petals)
12 x 5 cm x 5 cm pieces light yellow (B petals)
6 x 5.5 cm x 5.5 cm pieces light yellow (C petals)
1 x 5.5 cm x 5.5 cm piece yellow-green (chalice)
11 x 2.5 cm x 4 cm pieces yellow-green (leaves)

Other supplies

1 x 36 cm length of 0.8 mm steel wire (flower)
11 x 18 cm lengths of 0.3 mm steel wire (leaves)
Green floral ribbon

① Make the heart.

1

Overlay the A, B and C hearts, then sew the centre ((1) on the template).

2

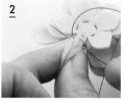

Pinch the bottom of the petal and sew ((2) on the template).

3

Sew the bottom of the other petals in the same manner.

4

(wrong side)

Turn over. Sew centre ((3) on the template). Stitch into 1st stitch.

5

Pull the thread to tighten.

6

The heart is complete.

② Make the flower. P (see p. 39)

1

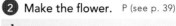

| A corolla/4 A petals | B corolla/5 B petals | B' corolla/7 B petals | C corolla/6 C petals |

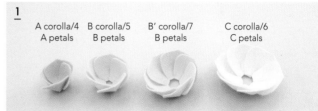

Assemble petals of the same size to form a cup.

2

Apply glue to the bottom of the heart, then glue the heart to the A corolla.

3

Apply glue to the bottom of the A corolla, then glue the A corolla to the B corolla.

4

Glue the C, then the D corollas in the same manner.

③ Glue the chalice.
K (see p. 37)

1

Make a circular support of 1.5 cm in diameter with 1 length of wire.

④ Make the leaves.

R (see p. 40)

2

Punch 1 hole in the centre of the chalice, then insert the wire from step 3-1. Glue the chalice to the back of the flower.

E (see p. 35)

Punch 1 hole through the thickness of the felt, then insert and glue 1 length of wire. Make 11 leaves. Assemble the leaves to make the following components: 1 component with 5 leaves, 2 components with 3 leaves.

⑤ Assemble the flower and the leaves.
S (see p. 40)

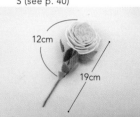

12cm

19cm

Join the flower and the leaves by wrapping floral ribbon around them. Cut excess wire and cover ends with floral ribbon.

88. Tea Rose P. 27

Supplies
Felt
1 x 6.5 cm x 6.5 cm piece dark red (heart)
3 x 4 cm x 4.5 cm pieces dark orange (A petals)
5 x 4.5 cm x 5 cm pieces orange (B petals)
1 x 5.5 cm x 5.5 cm piece green (chalice)
8 x 3 cm x 4.5 cm pieces green (leaves)

Other supplies
1 x 36 cm length of 0.8 mm steel wire (flower)
8 x 18 cm lengths of 0.3 mm steel wire (leaves)
Green floral ribbon

Full-size templates on p. 124.

1 Make the heart.

1
Apply glue to the edge of a heart petal, on the wrong side.

2
Curve the edge of the petal outward with a skewer.

3
Pin and leave to dry. Remove the skewer.

4
Curve the edge of the petals on either side in the same manner.

5
Turn over. Apply glue to the bottom of a petal that has not been curved.

6
Roll up the petal, pin and leave to dry.

7
Apply glue to the bottom of the next uncurved petal and roll it around the petal from step 1-6.

8
Pin and leave to dry.

2 Make the petals.

9
Apply glue to the bottom of the other petals and roll them around the component in the same manner.

10
The heart is complete.

1
Apply glue to the edge of the A petal, on the wrong side.

2
Curve the edge of the petal outward as per steps 1-2 and 3. Make 3 petals.

Continued p. 127.

N (see p. 38)

3

4

5

Apply glue to the end of the B petal, on the wrong side. Fold in 2 and hold in place with a clamp.

Curve the petal with a skewer as in step 2-2.

Pin and leave to dry. Make 5 petals.

❸ Make the flower.
P (see p. 39)

1

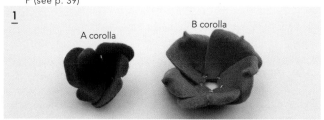

2

3

Sew 3 A petals forming a cup. Sew the 5 B petals in the same manner.

Apply glue to the bottom of the heart.

Glue the heart in the centre of the A petals.

4

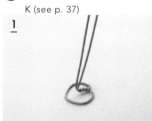

❹ Glue the chalice.
K (see p. 37)

1

R (see p. 40)

2

❺ Make the leaves.
E (see p. 35)

1

Apply glue to the bottom of the component from step 3-3, then glue it in the centre of the B petals.

Make a circular support of 1.3 cm in diameter with 1 length of wire.

Punch 1 hole in the centre of the chalice, then insert the wire from step 1. Glue the chalice to the back of the flower.

Punch 1 hole through the thickness of the felt, then insert and glue 1 length of wire. Make 8 leaves.

❻ Assemble the flower and the leaves.
S (see p. 40)

2

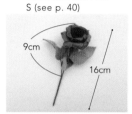

Assemble 3 leaves and wrap in floral ribbon. Make another component with 5 leaves.

Join the flower and the leaves by wrapping floral ribbon around them. Cut excess wire and cover ends with floral ribbon.

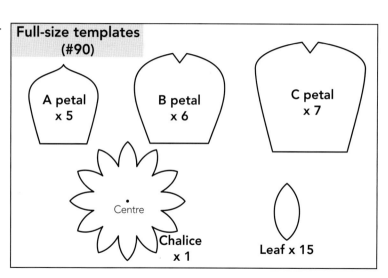

Full-size templates (#90)

A petal x 5

B petal x 6

C petal x 7

Chalice x 1 — Centre

Leaf x 15

127

90. China Rose P. 27

Supplies

Felt

5 x 3 cm x 3 cm pieces pink (A petals)

6 x 3.5 cm x 3.5 cm pieces light pink (B petals)

7 x 4 cm x 4 cm pieces light pink (C petals)

1 x 4 cm x 4 cm piece light green (chalice)

1.5 x 1.5 cm x 2.5 cm pieces light green (leaves)

Other supplies

1 x 36 cm length of 0.5 mm steel wire (flower)

15 x 18 cm lengths of 0.3 mm steel wire (leaves)

Green floral ribbon

Full-size templates on p. 127.

1 Make the heart.

O (see p. 39)

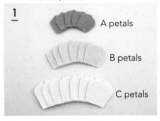

1

A petals

B petals

C petals

Assemble the petals of the same size as in the image above.

2

Roll up the A petals, followed by the B petals, then the C petals. Sew the bottom in a cross shape.

2 Glue the chalice.

K (see p. 37), R (see p. 40)

1

Make a circular support of 1.3 cm in diameter with 1 length of wire. Punch 1 hole in the centre of the chalice, then insert the wire. Apply glue.

2

Glue the chalice to the back of the flower.

3 Make the leaves.

E (see p. 35)

1

Punch 1 hole through the thickness of the felt, then insert and glue 1 length of wire. Make 15 leaves.

2

Assemble 5 leaves and wrap in floral ribbon. Make 3 identical components and wrap them in floral ribbon.

4 Assemble the flower and the leaves.

S (see p. 40)

6.5cm

11.5cm

Join the flower and the leaves by wrapping floral ribbon around them. Cut excess wire and cover ends with floral ribbon.

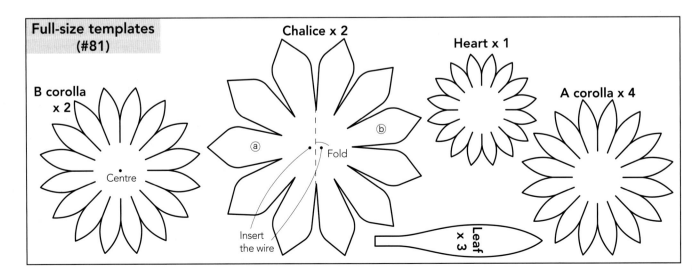

Full-size templates (#81)

Chalice x 2

Heart x 1

B corolla x 2

A corolla x 4

Centre

ⓐ

ⓑ

Fold

Insert the wire

Leaf x 3

91. Miniature Rose P. 27

Supplies

Felt

5 x 2 cm x 2 cm pieces light maroon (A petals)

6 x 3 cm x 3 cm pieces light maroon (B petals)

7 x 3 cm x 4 cm pieces beige (C petals)

1 x 4 cm x 4 cm piece dark green (chalice)

9 x 2 cm x 3 cm pieces dark green (leaves)

Other supplies

1 x 36 cm length of 0.8 mm steel wire (flower)

9 x 18 cm lengths of 0.3 mm steel wire (leaves)

Green floral ribbon

Full-size templates on p. 115.

① Make the heart.

O (see p. 39)

1

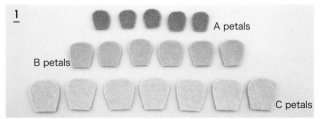

A petals

B petals

C petals

Cut 5 A petals, 6 B petals and 7 C petals.

2

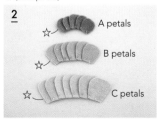

A petals

B petals

C petals

Assemble the petals of the same size horizontally.

3

Roll up the A petals starting from ☆, then sew the bottom in a cross shape (see p. 36).

4

Roll the B petals around the A petals starting from ☆.

5

Sew the bottom in a cross shape.

6

Roll the C petals in the same manner and sew the bottom in a cross shape.

② Glue the chalice.

K (see p. 37), R (see p. 40)

1

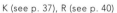

Make a circular support of 1 cm in diameter with 1 length of wire. Punch 1 hole in the centre of the chalice, then insert the wire and glue together.

2

Glue the chalice to the bottom of the flower.

③ Make the leaves.

E (see p. 35)

1

Punch 1 hole through the thickness of the felt, then insert and glue 1 length of wire. Make 3 leaves. Wrap the floral ribbon around the stem of 1 leaf.

2

Join the 2 other leaves, continuing to wrap in floral ribbon. Make 3 identical components.

④ Assemble the flower and the leaves.

S (see p. 40)

8cm

12.5cm

Join the flower and the leaves by wrapping floral ribbon around them. Cut excess wire and cover ends with floral ribbon.

92. English Rose P. 27

Supplies

Felt

1 x 5 cm x 5 cm piece orange red (heart)

4 x 3.5 cm x 4 cm pieces orange red (A petals)

5 x 3.5 cm x 4 cm pieces dark orange (B petals)

6 x 4 cm x 4 cm pieces orange (C petals)

1 x 4 cm x 4 cm pieces green (chalice)

5 x 2.5 cm x 4 cm pieces green (leaves)

Other supplies

1 x 36 cm length of 0.8 mm steel wire (flower)

5 x 18 cm lengths of 0.3 mm steel wire (leaves)

Green floral ribbon

Full-size templates on p. 52.

1 Make the heart.

1 Apply glue to 1 heart petal, then roll it up on itself.

2 Pin in place. Leave to dry.

3 Apply glue to the next petal.

4 Glue the next parts of the heart in the same manner.

2 Make the flower. P (see p. 39)

A corolla B corolla C corolla

1 Assemble the petals of the same size to form a cup.

2 Apply glue to the bottom of the heart, then glue the heart to the A corolla.

3 Apply glue to the bottom of the A corolla, then glue it to the B corolla. Glue the C corolla in the same manner.

3 Glue the chalice.

K (see p. 37), R (see p. 40)

Make a circular support of 1 cm in diameter with 1 length of wire. Punch 1 hole in the centre of the chalice, then insert the wire. Glue the chalice to the bottom of the flower.

4 Make the leaves.

E (see p. 35)

Punch 1 hole through the thickness of the felt, then insert and glue 1 length of wire. Make 5 leaves and assemble them by wrapping them in floral ribbon.

5 Assemble the flower and the leaves.

S (see p. 40)

16.5cm   8.5cm

Join the flower and the leaves by wrapping floral ribbon around them. Cut excess wire and cover ends with floral ribbon.

93. False Anemone P. 28

Supplies
Felt
6 x 3 cm x 3 cm pieces white (corolla)
3 x 3 cm x 3 cm pieces purple (hearts)
5 x 3 cm x 3 cm pieces light green (buds)
3 x 5 cm x 7 cm pieces yellow-green (leaves)

Full-size templates below.

Other supplies
3 x 0.3 cm purple beads (hearts)
3 x 0.6 cm x 0.9 cm wooden beads (hearts)
5 x 0.3 cm yellow-green beads (buds)
5 x 0.6 cm x 0.9 cm wooden beads (buds)
3 x 36 cm lengths of 0.55 mm steel wire (flowers)
5 x 36 cm lengths of 0.3 mm steel wire (buds)
3 x 18 cm lengths of 0.3 mm steel wire (leaves)
Green floral ribbon

---

1 Make the hearts.
B-1 (see p. 33), C-2 (see p. 34)

Thread 1 purple bead onto 1 length of wire and fold the wire in 2. Thread 1 wooden bead, then glue in place. Punch 1 hole in the centre of the heart, insert the wire and glue in place.

2 Make the flowers.
N (see p. 38)

1

Apply glue to the edge of the petals. Pinch to glue together. Make 2 components.

R (see p. 40)

2

Punch 1 hole in the centre of the corolla, insert the heart wire, then glue together. Glue another corolla, staggering the petals. Make 3 flowers.

3 Make the buds.
B-2 (see p. 33), C-2 (see p. 34)

Thread 1 green bead onto 1 length of wire, then twist the wire 2 or 3 times close to the bead. Thread the wooden bead, then glue in place. Punch 1 hole in the centre of the bud, insert the bead wire and glue in place. Make 5 buds.

---

4 Make the leaves.
E (see p. 35)

Punch 1 hole through the thickness of the felt, then insert and glue 1 length of wire. Make 3 leaves.

5 Assemble the flower, buds, and leaves.
S (see p. 40)

1

Assemble 1 flower and 2 buds and wrap in floral ribbon. Make another identical component. Make a component with 1 flower and 1 bud.

2

Assemble the 3 components from step 5-1 and wrap in floral ribbon.

3

12cm

19cm

Join the leaves to the component from step 5-2 and wrap in floral ribbon. Cut excess wire and cover ends with floral ribbon.

Full-size templates (#93)

Heart x 3
Bud x 5

Centre

Corolla x 6

Centre

Leaf x 3

94. Snowdrop P. 28

Supplies

Felt

3 x 6 cm x 6 cm pieces off-white (corollas)

3 x 4 cm x 4 cm pieces yellow-green (hearts)

3 x 3.5 cm x 3.5 cm pieces yellow-green (A chalices)

3 x 1.5 cm x 3 cm pieces yellow-green (B chalices)

5 x 2.5 cm x 6 cm pieces yellow-green (leaves)

Full-size templates on p. 113.

Other supplies

3 x 0.3 cm purple beads (hearts)

3 x 0.6 cm x 0.9 cm beige wooden beads (hearts)

3 x 0.6 cm x 0.9 cm beige wooden beads (chalices)

3 x 36 cm lengths of 0.45 mm steel wire (flowers)

3 x 18 cm lengths of 0.3 mm steel wire (B chalices)

5 x 18 cm lengths of 0.45 mm steel wire (leaves)

Green floral ribbon

1 Make the heart.

B-1 (see p. 33)

<u>1</u>

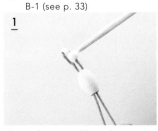

Thread 1 round bead onto 1 length of wire and fold the wire in 2. Thread 1 wooden bead onto the 2 strands of wire, then glue in place.

C-1 (see p. 34)

<u>2</u>

Punch 1 hole in the centre of the heart, then insert the wire from step 1-1. Glue in place.

2 Make the flower.

R (see p. 40)

<u>1</u>

Punch 1 hole in the centre of the corolla, then insert the heart wire. Apply glue.

<u>2</u>

Lift the petals, then glue in place. Make 3 flowers.

3 Glue the chalice.

<u>1</u>

Punch 1 hole in the centre of the A chalice, then insert the flower wire. Glue together.

C-1 (see p. 34)

<u>2</u>

Thread 1 wooden bead, then apply glue to the A chalice.

<u>3</u>

Glue in place.

E (see p. 35)

<u>4</u>

Punch 1 hole through the thickness of the B chalice, then insert and glue 1 length of wire. Make 3 identical components.

<u>5</u>

Assemble the components from steps 3-3 and 4 and wrap in floral ribbon.

<u>6</u>

Bend the stem at a 90-degree angle. Make 3 identical components.

4 Make the leaves.

E (see p. 35)

Punch 1 hole through the thickness of the felt, then insert and glue 1 length of wire. Make 5 leaves.

5 Assemble the flowers and the leaves.

S (see p. 40)

13cm

17cm

Join the flower and the leaves by wrapping floral ribbon around them. Cut excess wire and cover ends with floral ribbon.

96. Summer Snowflake P. 28

Supplies
Felt
6 x 5 cm x 5 cm pieces off-white (corollas)
6 x 4 cm x 4 cm pieces green (A chalices)
3 x 1.5 cm x 4 cm pieces green (B chalices)
5 x 3 cm x 10 cm pieces green (leaves)

Full-size templates on p. 106.

Other supplies
6 x 0.8 cm beige wooden beads (hearts)
6 x 0.6 cm beige wooden beads (A chalices)
6 x 18 cm lengths of 0.45 mm steel wire (pistils)
3 x 18 cm lengths of 0.45 mm steel wire (B chalices)
5 x 18 cm lengths of 0.45 mm steel wire (leaves)
Yellow #25 embroidery thread (pistils)
Green floral ribbon

1 Make the pistils.
Q (see p. 40)

1

Cut the embroidery thread into small pieces. Apply glue to 1 length of wire.

2

0.5cm

Glue embroidery thread to wire. Leave to dry.

3

Thread 1 wooden bead and glue in place.

2 Make the flower.
R (see p. 40)

1

Punch 1 hole in the centre of the corolla, then insert the heart wire. Apply glue to the bead, then glue every other petal.

2

Apply glue to the bottom of the remaining petals, then glue in place.

3 Glue the A chalice.

1

Punch 1 hole in the centre of the A chalice, then insert the flower wire. Apply glue.

C-1 (see p. 34)

2

Thread 1 wooden bead, then apply glue to the A chalice.

3

Glue in place. Make 6 components.

4 Make the B chalices and the leaves.
E (see p. 35)

B chalice — leaf

Punch 1 hole through the thickness of the felt, then insert and glue 1 length of wire. Make 3 B chalices and 5 leaves.

5 Assemble the flowers and the B chalices.

1

Assemble 2 flowers and 1 B chalice and wrap in floral ribbon.

2

Bend the flowers. Make 3 identical components.

6 Assemble the flowers and the leaves.
S (see p. 40)

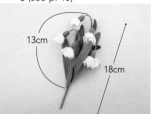

13cm

18cm

Join the flowers and the leaves by wrapping floral ribbon around them. Cut excess wire and cover ends with floral ribbon.

95. Lily of the Valley P. 28

Supplies
Felt
3 x 3 cm x 3 cm pieces off-white (A flowers)
3 x 3 cm x 3 cm pieces off-white (B flowers)
7 x 3.5 cm x 3.5 cm pieces off-white (C flowers)
4 x 5 cm x 12 cm pieces green (leaves)

Full-size templates on p. 108.

Other supplies
3 x 0.4 cm mother-of-pearl beads (A flowers)
3 x 0.4 cm mother-of-pearl beads (B flowers)
7 x 0.7 cm mother-of-pearl beads (C flowers)
13 x 18 cm lengths of 0.45 mm steel wire (flowers)
2 x 36 cm lengths of 0.45 mm steel wire (leaves)
Green floral ribbon

1 Make the B and C corollas.

A-1 (see p. 33)

1 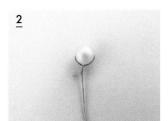	**2**	**3**	**4**

approximately 1 cm

1 Thread 1 bead onto 1 length of wire.

2 Twist the wire 2 or 3 times close to the bead.

3 Cut excess wire.

4 The heart is complete.

F-1 (see p. 35)   R (see p. 40)

5 	**6** 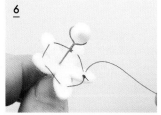	**7** 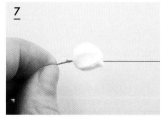	**8** 

5 Sew the C corolla, then stitch into the 1st stitch. Secure with a stop knot on the right side.

6 Punch 1 hole in the centre of the corolla, then insert the heart wire.

7 Pull the thread to tighten.

8 Secure with a stop knot, then insert it into the flower.

2 Make the A flowers.

A-1 (see p. 33)

9 	**10** 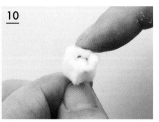	**11** 	**1** 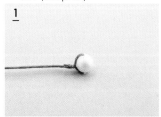

9 Apply glue to the edge of the flower.

10 Curve the ends of the petals outward. Leave to dry.

11 Make 7 C flowers. Make 3 B flowers in the same manner.

1 Thread 1 bead onto 1 length of wire. Twist the wire 2 or 3 times close to the bead, then cut excess wire.

Continued p. 135.

C-1 (see p. 34)

2

Punch 1 hole in the centre of the A corolla, then insert the wire from step 2-1. Apply glue to the corolla.

3

Glue the petals. Make 3 A flowers.

③ Assemble the flowers.

1

Assemble the A, B and C flowers and wrap in floral ribbon.

2

Position the flowers with tweezers.

3

6.5cm

The flower is complete.

④ Make the leaves.

1

Make the incisions with a rotary cutter.

2

Apply glue to the wrong side of the leaf.

3

2.5cm 8.5cm

Bend the wire into the shape of a leaf. Twist the wire 2 or 3 times at the base of the leaf.

4

Glue the wire to the leaf's wrong side.

5

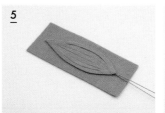

Glue a piece of 5 cm x 12 cm felt onto the component from step 4-4.

6

Cut around the shape. Place a weight onto the component for 20 minutes, allowing the glue to dry.

7

Bend the leaf into shape.

8

Make 2 leaves.

⑤ Assemble the flower and the leaves.
S (see p. 40)

12cm 18cm

Join the flower and the leaves by wrapping floral ribbon around them. Cut excess wire and cover ends with floral ribbon.

99. Queen of the Night P. 29

Full-size templates on p. 72.

Supplies

Felt

2 x 9 cm x 9 cm pieces white (A corollas)

1 x 9 cm x 9 cm piece white (B corolla)

1 x 11 cm x 11 cm piece white (C corolla)

1 x 1 cm x 2.5 cm piece white (A heart)

1 x 1 cm x 7 cm piece light yellow (B heart)

1 x 1.5 cm x 7.5 cm piece light yellow (C heart)

3 x 3 cm × 10 cm pieces green (leaves)

Other supplies

1 x 18 cm length of 0.8 mm steel wire (heart)

1 x 36 cm length of 0.8 mm steel wire (corolla)

3 x 18 cm lengths of 0.55 mm steel wire (leaves)

Green floral ribbon

1 Make the heart.

1

Notch the A heart over 0.5 cm, 0.3 cm apart. Stitch into the 1st stitch.

G-1 (see p. 36)

2

Pull the thread to tighten.

3

Insert 1 length of wire, then apply glue to its end.

4

Lift the A heart to glue it in place.

G-1 (see p. 36)

5

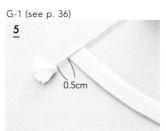

0.5cm

Notch the B heart over 0.5 cm, 0.3 cm apart. Apply glue and glue the length of wire.

H (see p. 36)

6

Roll up and glue in place.

G-1 (see p. 36)

7

Cut 1 long side of the C heart with the notching scissors, then notch. Apply glue to the unnotched side, then glue the B heart.

H (see p. 36)

8

Roll up and glue in place.

2 Make the flower.

F-1 (see p. 35)

1

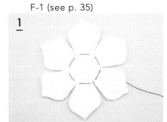

Sew the centre of the A corolla. Stitch into the 1st stitch.

R (see p. 40)

2

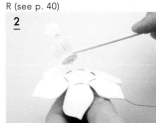

Punch 1 hole in the centre of the A corolla, then insert the heart wire. Apply glue to the side and bottom of the heart.

3

Glue together. Pull thread to tighten the corolla.

4

Glue another A corolla, staggering the petals.

5

Punch 1 hole in the centre of the B corolla, then insert the wire from step 2-4.

N (see p. 38)

6

Apply glue to the ends of the petals of the C corolla.

Continued p. 137.

7

Fold the ends of the petal in 2 and hold with clamps.

8

Leave to dry, then remove the clamps.

9

If necessary, cut the ends of the petals to remove excess glue.

K (see p. 37), R (see p. 40)

10

Make a circular support of 1.8 cm in diameter with 1 length of wire. Punch 1 hole in the centre of the C corolla, then insert the wire and glue in place.

③ Make the leaves.

E (see p. 35)

Punch 1 hole through the thickness of the felt, then insert and glue 1 length of wire. Make 3 leaves.

④ Assemble the flowers and the leaves.

S (see p. 40)

10.5cm

17.5cm

Join the flower and the leaves by wrapping floral ribbon around them. Cut excess wire and cover ends with floral ribbon.

11

Insert the wire from step 2-5 in the hole from step 2-10.

12

Glue together.

---

100. Calla P. 29

Full-size templates on p. 107.

Supplies
Felt
1 x 6 cm x 8 cm piece white (corolla)
1 x 1 cm x 20 cm piece yellow (heart)
1 x 3 cm x 4 cm piece yellow-green (chalice)
Other supplies
1 x 36 cm length of 0.55 mm steel wire (flower)
Green floral ribbon

① Make the heart.

G-1 (see p. 36), L (see p. 38)

1

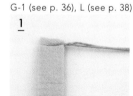

Notch the A heart over 0.5 cm, 0.3 cm apart. Attach the wire to the end, then twist the wire 2 or 3 times close to the edge of the felt.

② Make the flower.

I (see p. 37)

2

5cm

Apply glue and roll up the felt in a spiral.

1

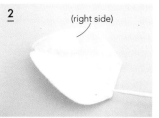

(wrong side)

Fold the corolla in 2, right sides facing, then sew the fold using overlock stitches.

2

(right side)

Apply glue to the bottom of the corolla.

3

Glue the corolla around the heart. Pin in place and leave to dry.

③ Glue the chalice.

1

Apply glue to the chalice.

2

Glue the chalice around the bottom of the flower.

④ Make the stem.

S (see p. 40)

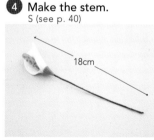

18cm

Wrap floral ribbon around the length of wire.

101. Lily P. 29

Full-size templates on p. 60.

Supplies
Felt
3 x 2.5 cm x 7 cm pieces off-white (A petals)
3 x 3.5 cm x 7 cm pieces off-white (B petals)
1 x 2.5 cm x 2.5 cm piece light green (pistil)
5 x 2.5 cm x 6.5 cm pieces yellow-green (leaves)

Other supplies
1 x 0.2 cm yellow bead (heart)
1 x 0.4 cm beige wooden bead (pistil)
6 x 18 cm lengths of white 0.3 mm steel wire (petals)
6 x 18 cm lengths of 0.3 mm steel wire (stamens)
1 x 36 cm length of 0.3 mm steel wire (pistil)
5 x 18 cm lengths of 0.45 mm steel wire (leaves)
Yellow #25 embroidery thread
Green floral ribbon

1 Make the stamens.
Q (see p. 40)

Cut the embroidery thread into small pieces.

Cut some more.

3

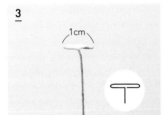

Bend 1 length of wire into a T shape, then apply glue.

4

Glue the cuts of thread onto the wire.

5

Leave to dry.

2 Make the pistils.
B-2 (see p. 33)

1

Thread 1 yellow bead onto 1 length of wire, then twist the wire 2 or 3 times. Thread 1 wooden bead onto the 2 strands, then glue in place.

2

Punch 1 hole in the centre of the heart, then insert the wire from step 2-1.

3 C-1 (see p. 34)

Glue the petals onto the bead.

3 Make the heart.

1

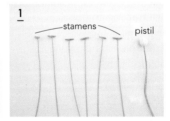

stamens — pistil

Make 6 stamens and 1 pistil.

2

Bend the T part of the stamens.

3

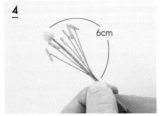

Wrap floral ribbon around the pistil stem.

4

Assemble the stamens around the pistil, then wrap in floral ribbon.

4 Make the petals.
I (see p. 37)

1

Fold the B petal, right sides facing, then sew using overlock stitches.

2 E (see p. 35)

Punch 1 hole through the thickness of the felt.

Continued p. 139.

3

Insert and glue 1 length of wire.

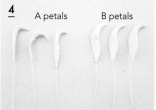

4 A petals   B petals

Make 3 A petals and 3 B petals.

1

Assemble the B petals around the heart.

2

Join the A petals around the component from step 5.1.

3

Wrap in floral ribbon, covering the bottom of the petals.

4

Shape the pistil.

⑥ **Make the leaves.**

E (see p. 35)

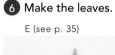

Punch 1 hole through the thickness of the felt, then insert and glue 1 length of wire. Make 5 leaves.

⑦ **Assemble the flowers and the leaves.**

S (see p. 40)

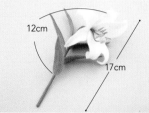

12cm

17cm

Join the flower and the leaves by wrapping floral ribbon around them. Cut excess wire and cover ends with floral ribbon.

---

97. Chamomile P. 29

Full-size templates below.

Supplies

Felt

14 x 3.5 cm x 3.5 cm pieces white (corollas)

3 x 3 cm x 4 cm pieces yellow-green (leaves)

Other supplies

7 x 36 cm lengths of 0.3 mm steel wire (hearts)

3 x 18 cm lengths of 0.3 mm steel wire (leaves)

7 x 1 cm yellow pompoms

Green floral ribbon

① **Make the hearts.**

K (see p. 37)

1

Make a circular support of 0.5 cm in diameter with 1 length of wire.

2

Apply glue to the support and glue 1 pompom.

② **Make the flower.**

R (see p. 40)

Punch 1 hole in the centre of the corolla, then insert the heart wire. Glue in place. Glue another corolla, staggering the petals. Make 7 flowers.

③ **Make the leaves.**

D (see p. 34)

Apply glue to the bottom of the leaf. Place the wire on the leaf and fold the leaf in 2. Make 3 leaves.

④ **Assemble the flowers and the leaves.**

S (see p. 40)

9cm

15cm

Join the flower and the leaves by wrapping floral ribbon around them. Cut excess wire and cover ends with floral ribbon.

Full-size template (#97)

Corolla x 14

Centre

Leaf x 3

98. Daffodil P. 29

Supplies
Felt
6 x 6 cm x 6 cm pieces off-white (corollas)
2 x 3.5 cm x 3.5 cm pieces off-white (buds)
15 x 2.5 cm x 3 cm pieces yellow (hearts)
5 x 2 cm x 10 cm pieces dark green (leaves)

Full-size templates p. 58.

Other supplies
2 x 0.3 cm yellow bead (buds)
2 x 0.6 cm × 0.9 cm beige wooden bead (buds)
3 x 36 cm lengths of 0.45 mm steel wire (flowers)
2 x 36 cm lengths of 0.45 mm steel wire (buds)
5 x 18 cm lengths of 0.45 mm steel wire (leaves)
Green floral ribbon

1 Make the hearts.
O (see p. 39)

Sew the 5 heart pieces. Roll up, then sew the bottom in a cross shape.

2 Make the flowers.
N (see p. 38)

1

Apply glue to the ends of the petals, then fold in 2. Hold with a clamp. Make 6 components.

K (see p. 37), R (see p. 40)

2

Make a circular support of 0.5 cm in diameter with 1 length of wire. Punch 1 hole in the centre of the corolla, then insert the wire. Make 3 components.

3

Apply glue to the side and bottom of the heart, then glue it to the corolla that is not on a wire.

4

Lift the petals. Pin and leave to dry.

5

Apply glue to the side and bottom of the component from step 2-4. Glue to the component from step 2-2.

6

Lift the petals. Pin and leave to dry. Make 3 flowers.

3 Make the buds.
B-1 (see p. 33), C-1 (see p. 34)

Thread 1 yellow bead and 1 wooden bead onto 1 length of wire. Punch 1 hole in the centre of the bud, then insert the wire. Glue together. Make 2 buds.

4 Make the leaves.
E (see p. 35)

Punch 1 hole through the thickness of the felt, then insert and glue 1 length of wire. Make 5 leaves.

5 Assemble the flowers and the buds.

1

Wrap each bud and flower stem in floral ribbon. Bend the stems.

2

Assemble the flowers and the buds and wrap in floral ribbon.

6 Assemble the flowers and the leaves.
S (see p. 40)

12.5cm
18cm

Join the component from step 5-2 and the leaves by wrapping floral ribbon around them. Cut excess wire and cover ends with floral ribbon.

Supplies and Materials

Below are the supplies and materials used in this book.

Supplies

Felt

20 cm x 20 cm felt pieces, 1 mm thick. Composition: 60% wool, 40% rayon. Available in a wide variety of colours.

Floral Ribbon

Wrap around the stems to hold them in place. It comes in a wide variety of colours.

Lengths of Steel wire to Make Stems

Lengths of wire covered in ribbon. 0.8 mm, 0.55 mm, 0.45 mm, 0.37 mm, and 0.3 mm in diameter.

Pompoms

For the heart and for the mimosa flower.

Beads

From left to right: 0.2 cm round beads, 0.3 cm round beads, wooden beads, mother-of-pearl beads. Used for hearts, corollas, or buds.

Embroidery Thread

Cut into small pieces to make the hearts.

Sewing Thread

To sew corollas and beads. Choose a color that matches the felt.

Materials

Paper

To make the templates.

Pen

To trace the templates.

Markers

To trace the templates onto the felt.

Tailor's Awl

To punch holes and to make tendrils. Have 2 different sizes on hand.

Glue

Choose a glue that is adapted to felt.

Tweezers

To shape certain components.

Tailor Scissors

To cut the felt.

Notching Scissors

To create 0.3 cm zigzags.

Cutting Pliers

To cut the steel wire.

Flat or Round Pliers

To bend the steel wire and thread the beads.

Needles

A large needle and an embroidery needle with a round head.

Small Scissors

To cut the embroidery thread.

Thread Cutter

To cut the thread.

Clamps

To hold glued pieces together while they dry.

Pins

To hold glued pieces while they dry.

Skewers

To apply glue and bend petals.

Egg Cup

To allow a textured flower to dry and give it a rounded shape.

Making the Brooches

See p. 41 for how to make a brooch with just one model.

Models on p. 30.

a

Size: 7.5 cm × 13 cm

Supplies

Sutera
Felt
7 x 3.5 cm x 3.5 cm pieces light yellow (corollas)
Other supplies
7 x 0.3 cm green beads (hearts)
7 x 36 cm lengths of 0.3 mm steel wire (flowers)

Dandelion
Felt
2 x 1.5 cm x 10 cm pieces yellow (A corollas)
2 x 1.7 cm x 15.3 cm pieces light yellow (B corollas)
2 x 3.5 cm x 3.5 cm pieces yellow-green (chalices)
3 x 2.5 cm x 7.5 cm pieces yellow-green (leaves)
Other supplies
2 x 36 cm lengths of 0.55 mm steel wire (flowers)
3 x 18 cm lengths of 0.55 mm steel wire (leaves)

Baby's Breath
Felt
36 x 2 cm x 2 cm pieces white (corollas)
Other supplies
18 x 36 cm lengths of 0.3 mm steel wire (flowers)
18 x 0.2 cm yellow beads (hearts)

Mimosa
Felt
5 x 3 cm x 4 cm pieces green (leaves)
Other supplies
20 x 18 cm lengths of 0.3 mm steel wire (flowers)
5 x 18 cm lengths of 0.3 mm steel wire (leaves)
20 x 0.8 cm yellow pompoms (flowers)
Green floral ribbon
1 x 3.5 cm wide brooch pin

Basic instructions

1 Make 18 baby's breath flowers (p. 58), 20 mimosa flowers and 5 mimosa leaves (p. 59), 2 a dandelion flowers and 3 a dandelion leaves (p. 55), and 7 sutera flowers (p. 88). Assemble components of the same model and wrap them in floral ribbon.

2 Place the open brooch pin on the mimosa stem and wrap in floral ribbon.

3 Join the component from step 2 and the dandelion and wrap in floral ribbon.

4 Join the baby's breath and the sutera to the component from step 3 and wrap in floral ribbon.

5 Cut the steel wires 15 cm from the flowers. Wrap in floral ribbon all the way to the end.

Supplies

Daffodil
Felt
4 x 6 cm x 6 cm pieces light yellow (corollas)
3 x 3.5 cm x 3.5 cm pieces light yellow (buds)
10 x 2.5 cm x 3 cm pieces yellow (hearts)
Other supplies
3 x 0.3 cm yellow beads (buds)
3 x 0.6 cm x 0.9 cm beige wooden beads (buds)
2 x 36 cm lengths of 0.45 mm steel wire (flowers)
3 x 36 cm lengths of 0.45 mm steel wire (buds)

Myosotis
Felt
12 x 2 cm x 2 cm pieces light blue (corollas)
5 x 2 cm x 6 cm pieces green (leaves)
Other supplies
12 x 0.3 cm light yellow beads (hearts)
12 x 36 cm lengths of 0.3 mm steel wire (flowers)
5 x 18 cm lengths of 0.3 mm steel wire (leaves)

French Marigold
Felt
3 x 1.5 cm x 4.8 cm pieces purple (corollas)
3 x 3 cm x 3 cm pieces orange (hearts)

Other supplies
3 x 36 cm lengths of 0.3 mm steel wire (flowers)
Green floral ribbon
1 x 3.5 cm wide brooch pin

Instructions

1. Assemble 2 daffodil flowers and 3 daffodil buds (p. 140) and 3 French marigold flowers (p. 45) and wrap them in floral ribbon.
2. Place the open brooch pin on the stem from step 1 and wrap in floral ribbon.
3. Make 1 component with 2 myosotis leaves and 1 component with 3 myosotis leaves (p. 42).
4. Assemble the components from steps 2 and 3 and wrap them in floral ribbon.
5. Assemble 12 myosotis flowers (p. 42) and wrap them in floral ribbon.
6. Assemble the components from steps 4 and 5 and wrap them in floral ribbon.
7. Cut the steel wires 12.5 cm from the flowers. Wrap in floral ribbon all the way to the end.

b

Size: 12,5 cm × 5 cm

c

Size: 9.5 cm × 10 cm

Supplies

Feverfew

Felt

6 x 4 cm x 4 cm pieces light pink (corollas)

9 x 3 cm x 3 cm pieces light yellow (hearts)

3 x 3.5 cm x 4 cm pieces light green (leaves)

Other supplies

3 x 36 cm lengths of 0.3 mm steel wire (flowers)

3 x 18 cm lengths of 0.3 mm steel wire (leaves)

Baby's Breath

Felt

14 x 2 cm x 2 cm pieces light grey (corollas)

Other supplies

7 x 0.2 cm light green beads (flowers)

7 x 36 cm lengths of 0.3 mm steel wire (flowers)

Jasmine

Felt

6 x 3.5 cm x 3.5 cm pieces light blue (corollas)

2 x 3 cm x 5 cm pieces green (leaves)

Other supplies

3 x 0.3 cm light yellow beads (flowers)

3 x 36 cm lengths of 0.3 mm steel wire (flowers)

2 x 18 cm lengths of 0.3 mm steel wire (leaves)

Green floral ribbon

1 x 2.8 cm wide brooch pin

Instructions

1. Assemble 3 feverfew flowers and 3 feverfew leaves (p. 56) and wrap them in floral ribbon.

2. Place the open brooch pin on the stem and wrap in floral ribbon.

3. Join 7 baby's breath flowers (p. 58), 3 jasmine flowers and 2 jasmine leaves (p. 56) to the component from step 2. Wrap in floral ribbon.

4. Cut the steel wires 10 cm from the flowers. Wrap in floral ribbon all the way to the end.

d

Size: 6 cm × 12.5 cm

Supplies

China Rose

Felt

5 x 3 cm x 3 cm pieces red (A corollas)

6 x 3.5 cm x 3.5 cm pieces coral (B corollas)

7 x 4 cm x 4 cm pieces pink (C corollas)

1 x 4 cm x 4 cm piece light green (chalice)

15 x 1.5 cm x 2.5 cm pieces light green (leaves)

Other supplies

1 x 36 cm length of 0.55 mm steel wire (flowers)

15 x 18 cm lengths of 0.3 mm steel wire (leaves)

Anemone Pseudoaltaica

Felt

10 x 3 cm x 3 cm pieces violet (corollas)

Other supplies

5 x 36 cm lengths of 0.3 mm steel wire (flowers)

5 x 0.3 cm pink beads (flowers)

Silver Ragwort

Felt

2 x 3 cm x 3 cm yellow (bud hearts)

2 x 3 cm x 3 cm yellow (bud corollas)

2 x 3 cm x 3 cm yellow-green (chalice)

3 x 3 cm x 3 cm yellow (flower hearts)

6 x 3.5 cm x 3.5 cm off-white (flower corollas)

Other supplies

2 x 36 cm lengths of 0.3 mm steel wire (buds)

3 x 36 cm lengths of 0.3 mm steel wire (flowers)

Green floral ribbon

1 x 3.5 cm wide brooch pin

Instructions

1. Assemble 1 China rose flower and 1 China rose leaf (p. 128), 5 anemone pseudoaltaica flowers (p. 48), and 3 silver ragwort flowers and 2 silver ragwort buds (p. 57). Wrap each model in floral ribbon.

2. Cut steel wires 13 cm from flowers.

3. Join the China rose and anemone pseudoaltaica and wrap them in floral ribbon.

4. Cut steel wires 12.5 cm from flowers.

5. Join the component from step 4 and the silver ragwort. Wrap in floral ribbon.

6. Place the open brooch pin on the stem and wrap in floral ribbon.

7. Wrap the silver ragwort stem around a punch to create the tendrils.

e

Size: 7 cm × 11 cm

Supplies

Spanish Needles

Felt

6 x 3.5 cm x 3.5 cm pieces beige (corollas)

3 x 3 cm x 3 cm pieces light maroon (hearts)

Other supplies

3 x 36 cm lengths of 0.3 mm steel wire (flowers)

Blue Daisy

Felt

2 x 2.5 cm x 3.5 cm pieces light grey (corollas)

6 x 2 cm x 3 cm pieces maroon (leaves)

Other supplies

2 x 0.8 cm purple pompoms (hearts)

2 x 36 cm lengths of 0.45 mm steel wire (flowers)

6 x 18 cm lengths of 0.3 mm steel wire (leaves)

Dahlia (leaves)

Felt

1 x 3.5 cm x 4.5 cm piece light grey (A leaf)

2 x 2.5 cm x 3.5 cm pieces light grey (B leaves)

2 x 3 cm x 4.5 cm pieces light grey (C leaves)

Other supplies

5 x 18 cm lengths of 0.3 mm steel wire (leaves)

Grey floral ribbon

1x 2.8 cm wide brooch pin

Instructions

1. Make 3 Spanish needles flowers (p. 58), 2 components with 2 blue daisy flowers and 3 blue daisy leaves (p.45), and 1 dahlia leaf (p. 116). Assemble all the components and wrap them in floral ribbon.

2. Place the open brooch pin on the stem and wrap in floral ribbon.

3. Cut steel wires 11 cm from flowers and wrap in floral ribbon all the way to the end.

Tuva Publishing
www.tuvapublishing.com

Address Merkez Mah. Cavusbasi Cad. No71
Cekmekoy - Istanbul 34782 / Turkey
Tel +9 0216 642 62 62

101 Beautiful Felt Flowers

First Print 2021 / October

All Global Copyrights Belong To
Tuva Tekstil ve Yayıncılık Ltd.

Content Felt

Editor in Chief Ayhan DEMİRPEHLİVAN
Project Editor Kader DEMİRPEHLİVAN
Author Pieni SIENI
Technical Editors Leyla ARAS
Graphic Designers Ömer ALP, Abdullah BAYRAKÇI,
Tarık TOKGÖZ
Translator Julie DESJARDINS

ISBN 978-605-7834-24-9

Lady Boutique Series No.4879
Felt de Tsukuru Otona no Hana 101
Copyright © Boutique-sha, Inc. 2019
Original Japanese edition published in Japan by
Boutique-sha, Inc.
English translation rights arranged with Boutique-sha, Inc.

  TuvaYayincilik Ⓟ TuvaPublishing
 TuvaYayincilik Ⓘ TuvaPublishing